AF885245

Computer FUNdamentals

Know it Sooner
Computer Training

www.knowitsooner.com
780-940-6772
info@knowitsooner.com

January 2022
December 2025

Table of Contents

Getting to Know the Keyboard

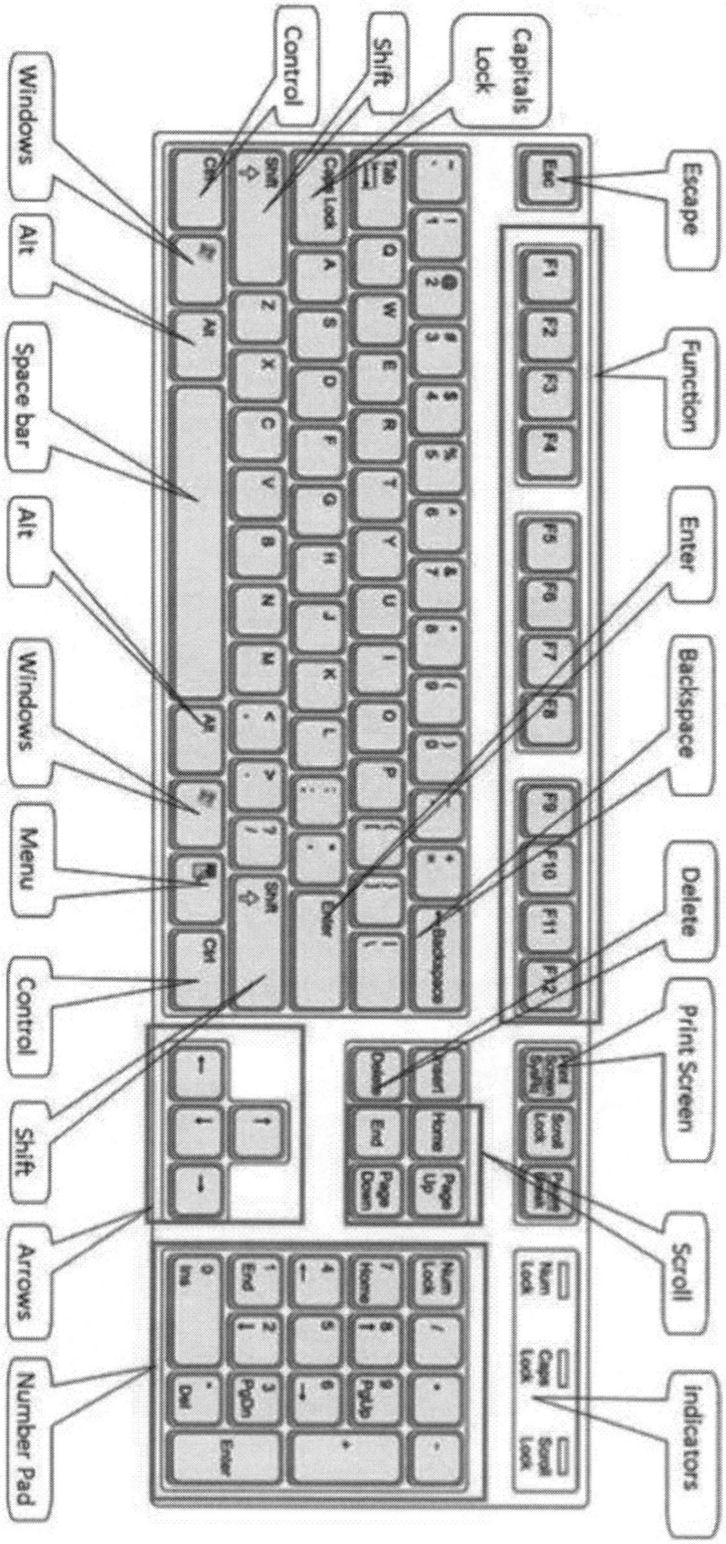

Starting Programs

You will see some icons on your desktop that will start programs. You'll see some on your taskbar as well. If it's on your desktop, you must double click on it to start it. Otherwise, you only need to click once.

If you can't see the program you're looking for, click other Start button on the bottom left corner of the screen and look in the program list.

The Desktop

You will see icons on your desktop and buttons on your taskbar for some of the programs on your computer. You will need to double click on the icons on the desktop and single click the others. If you can't see the program you're looking for, click on the start menu in the bottom right corner of the screen.

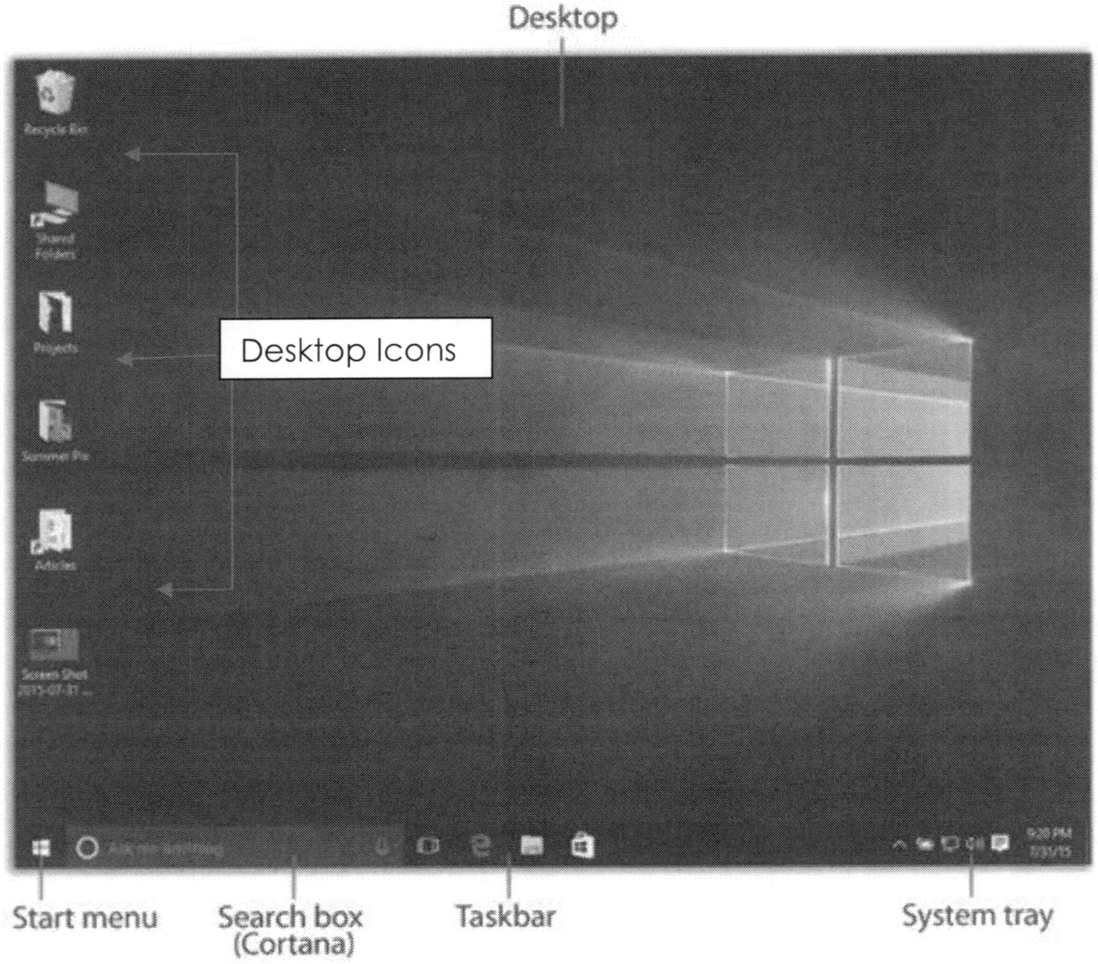

The Program Window

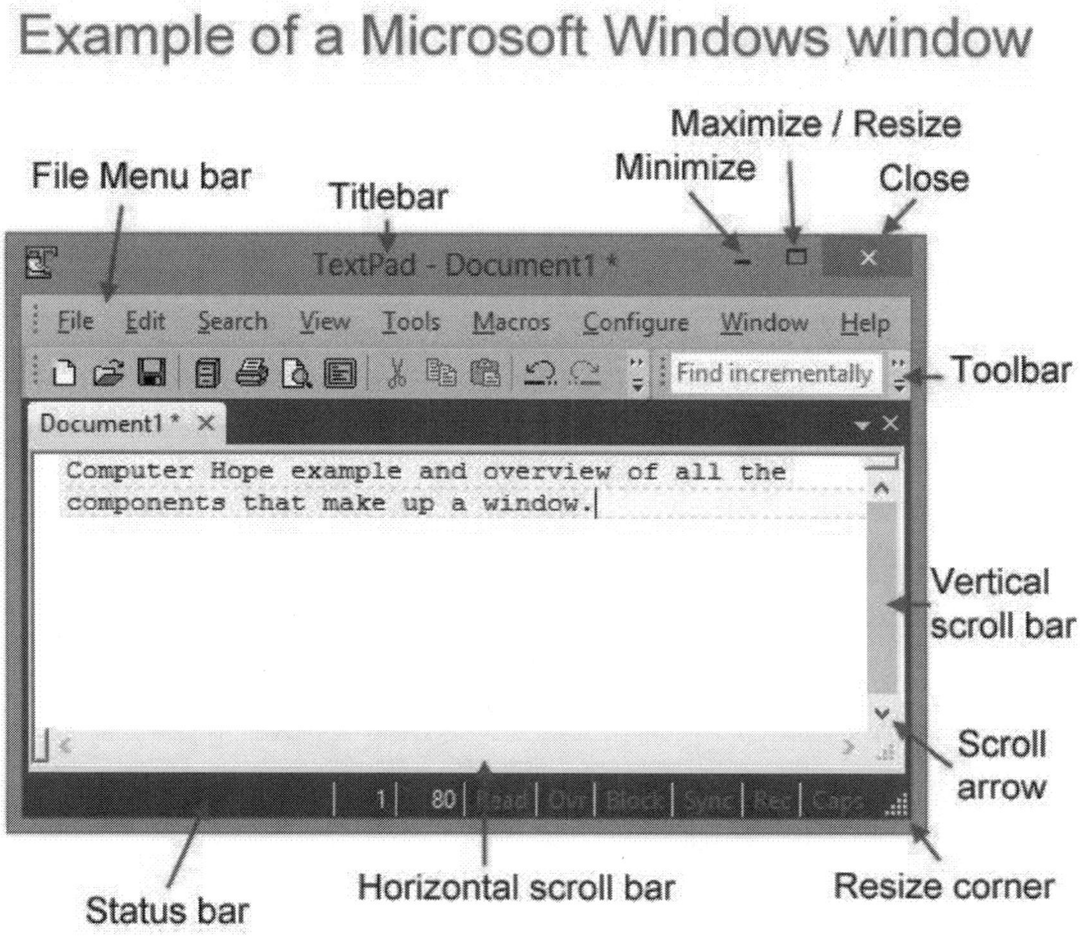

The three buttons on the top right corner are consistent in most program windows.

Minimize – hides the window without closing it. Simply bring it up again by clicking on its icon on the taskbar. It likely has a white line underneath it to indicate it is currently running.

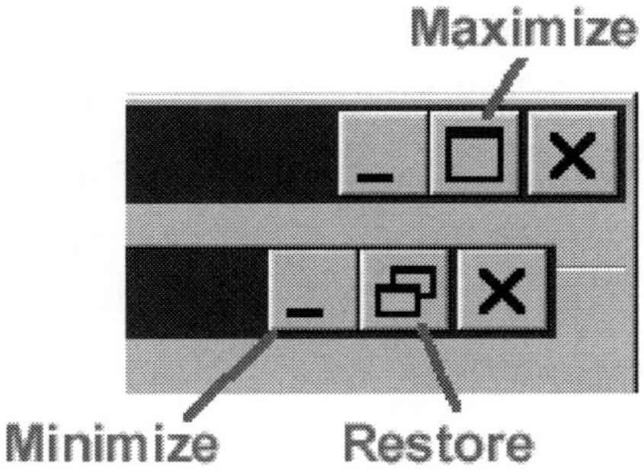

Maximize – this will make the window nearly as large as the computer screen so you can't see the desktop or any other programs that are currently running. When you click on this, you will then see a Restore button in it's place which will make the window the size it was before it was maximized.

Close – this closes the window and usually ends the program. You must find the icon you used to initially open this program in order to use it again.

Programs

Type of Program	Name of Program	Uses
Browser	Internet Explorer Microsoft Edge Google Chrome	Browse websites, check email
Word Processor	Microsoft Word (Part of Microsoft Office) Google Docs	Create letters, reports, signs, manuals, resumes, business cards
Spreadsheet	Microsoft Excel (Part of Microsoft Office) Google Sheets	Create budgets, worksheets, reports, graphs and lists with mathematical functions
Presentations	Microsoft PowerPoint (Part of Microsoft Office) Prezi Google Slides	Create presentations for sales, training, etc. as well as picture slide shows and signs
Email	Outlook Windows Mail	Use Email, Calendar, Contacts
AI	ChatGPT, Claude, Gemini, Copilot	Programs that help you write, learn, and get answers by typing questions in plain language. They can help with emails, documents, ideas, and problem-solving.
PDF Reader	Adobe Reader	To read reports that are sent to you in PDF format
File Management	File Explorer (yellow folder on your taskbar)	Create folders, move, copy, rename delete files (documents, pictures, etc.)
Accessory Programs (Free with Windows) Available by clicking on Start button at the bottom of screen	Calculator Paint Word Pad Solitaire Photos Windows Media Player	

The Internet

The World Wide Web consists of:

- Your **personal computer**
- **Web browser software** to access the Web
- A connection to an **Internet service provider** (ISP). Common ones are Shaw and Telus.
- **Servers** to host the data
- **Routers** and **switches** to direct the flow of data

Internet Terminology

World Wide Web	A part of the internet that let's you jump from site to site.
E-mail	A mail accessory that sends mail over the Internet.
Web Site	A series of pages (web pages) that an individual or organization creates and displays on the internet for others to see.
Online	When your computer is connected to the Internet.
Network	A bunch of computers attached together to share information and programs. It used to be that networks were only in the workplace but now people are creating them in their homes to share their internet connection, files, and printers.
Internet Explorer (Browser Software)	The program most commonly used for "surfing the internet". It is referred to as a browser program.
Link	A part of a webpage that takes the user to another place on the internet when clicked on (could be another webpage or an email). It is sometimes underlined, but not always. Your cursor changes to a hand when it is overtop of a link. 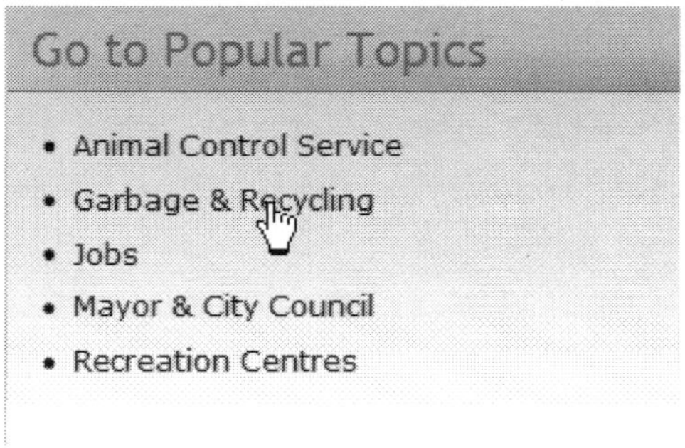
URL or website address	Each page has a unique address known as a **URL** (Uniform Resource Locator), which identifies its location on the server. Ie. www.knowitsooner.com

Websites

- A **website** consists of one or more web pages that relate to a common theme, such as a person, business, organization, or a subject, such as news or sports.
- The first page is called the **home page**, which acts like an index, indicating the content on the site.
- From the home page, you can click **links** to access other pages on the site or other resources on the Web.

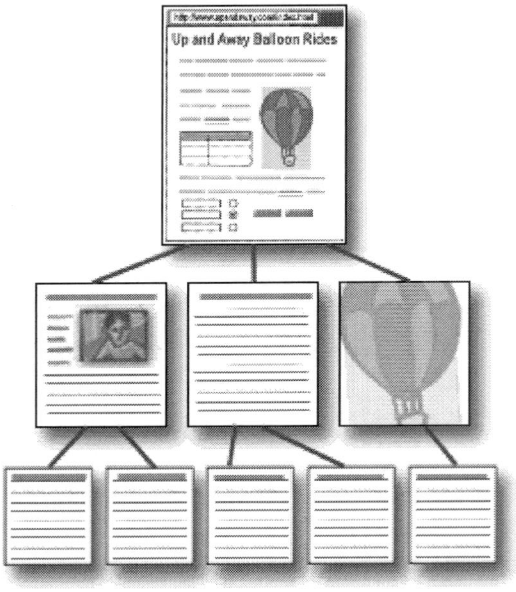

Accessing the Internet

Double Click on the icon that is the browser on your computer. It will likely be one of the following programs

- Internet Explorer
- Microsoft Edge
- Google Chrome

Ways to find Information on the Internet

Type the Address

1. Click in the address bar at the top
2. Type the address (URL) if you know it.
3. Press ENTER.
4. If you have typed the address correctly, it will take you directly there.

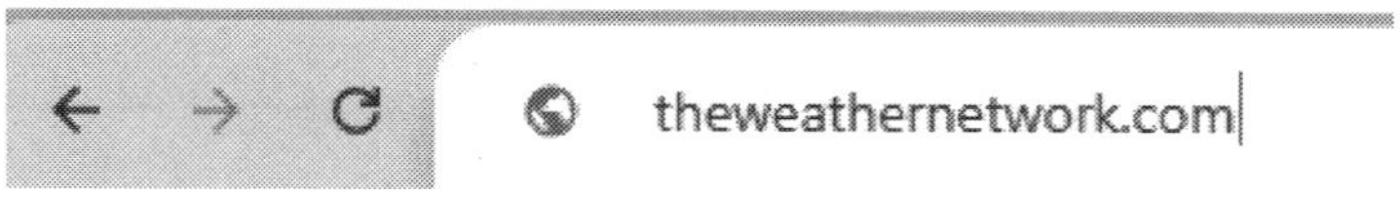

Search for it

If you don't know the address, you can search for it.

1. In the address bar, type in the search terms.
2. Press ENTER.
3. It will guess what you want and list matches or "hits". You can click on any of the suggestions.

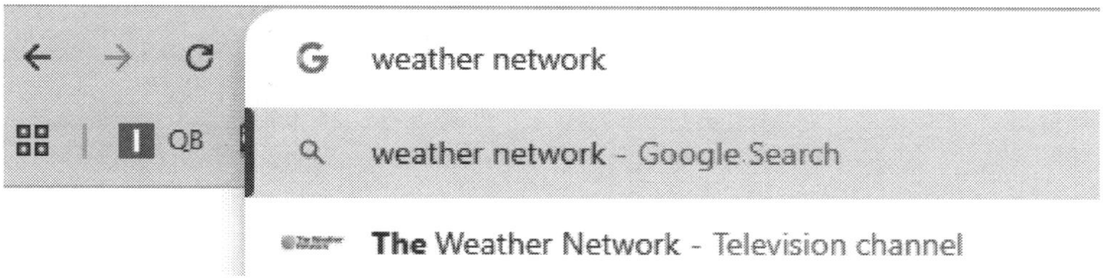

If it brings up too many choices, try putting the term in quotes. Then it will only search for that exact phrase. (ie. "weather network"). It will then only list websites with that exact phrase.

Click on a Link

If you see some text or an image that makes the cursor change into a hand, click on it and it will take you to a webpage!

Sometimes you just left click on it, other times you hold the CTRL key down as well.

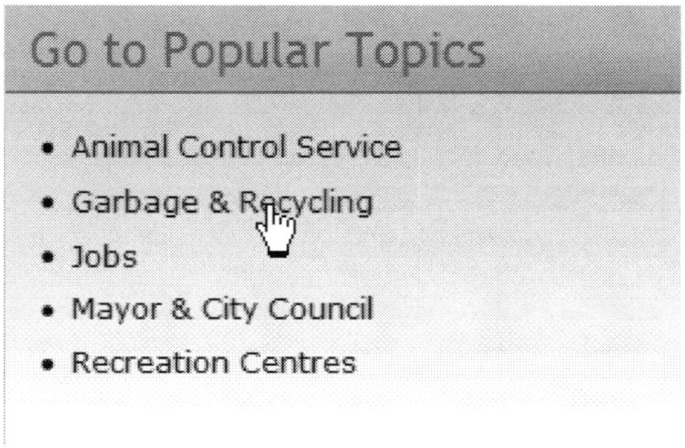

Cool Websites

AI
chatgpt.com
copilot.microsoft.com
claude.ai
gemini.google.com

Buy and Sell
buysell.com
craigslist.com
kijiji.ca
marketplace.facebook.com

City of Edmonton Website
edmonton.ca

Dictionary
dictionary.com
urbandictionary.com

Education
coursera.org
duolingo.com
gcflearnfree.org
khanacademy.org
knowitsooner.com
skillshare.com
ted.com

Email
gmail.com
outlook.com

Encyclopaedia
wikipedia.org
wolframalpha.com

Entertainment/Music/Events
eventbrite.ca
gutenberg.org
imdb.com
libby.app
pinterest.com
radio.garden
spotify.com
youtube.com

Fact Checker/Security
consumer.ftc.gov
seniorfraudalert.ca
snopes.com

Fun and Games
akinator.com
autodraw.com
boredbutton.com
earthcam.com
jigidi.com
rainymood.com
solitaired.com
sporcle.com
theuselessweb.com
websudoku.com
window-swap.com
worldguessr.com

Job Hunting Websites
indeed.com
kijiji.ca
monster.com
workopolis.com

Medical Information
webmd.com
albertahealthservices.ca
mayoclinic.org

News
canada.com
cnn.com
edmontonjournal.com
edmontonsun.com
taprootedmonton.com

Outdoors
alltrails.com
reserve.albertaparks.ca

Senior's Pages
seniors.gc.ca
elder.org
canadaliving.com
goodtimes.ca

Shopping
amazon.ca
costco.ca
redflagdeals.com

Social Media
facebook.com
instagram.com
linkedin.com
meetup.com
x.com

Sports
tsn.ca
edmontonoilers.com
goelks.com

Television Listings
tvguide.com

The Weather Network
theweathernetwork.com

Travel
aircanada.com
ebus.ca
googlemaps.com
redarrow.ca
tripadvisor.ca
westjet.com

Typing Practise
typing.com

World Currency Exchange Rates
xe.com

Favorites

Adding a Website to your Favorites

When you find a website that you want to save to access later, you can add to your favorites (Microsoft Edge) or bookmarks (Google Chrome) so you can easily find it again.

1. Click on the star to add this site to your favorites/bookmarks.

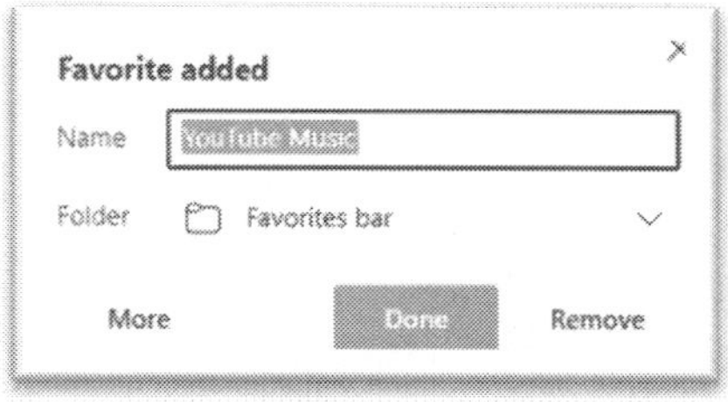

If you put it in the Favorites/Bookmarks bar, it will appear right on the toolbar.

If you can't see the toolbar, click on the three dots in the corner and click on Favorites. You will see all sorts of options to customize your favorites!

You can also put it in your general favorite/bookmark area. You can even create subfolders!

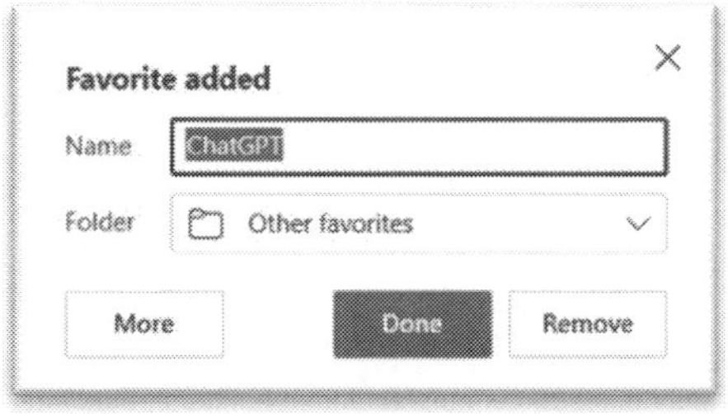

Click on the favorite/bookmark button to see everything you have saved.

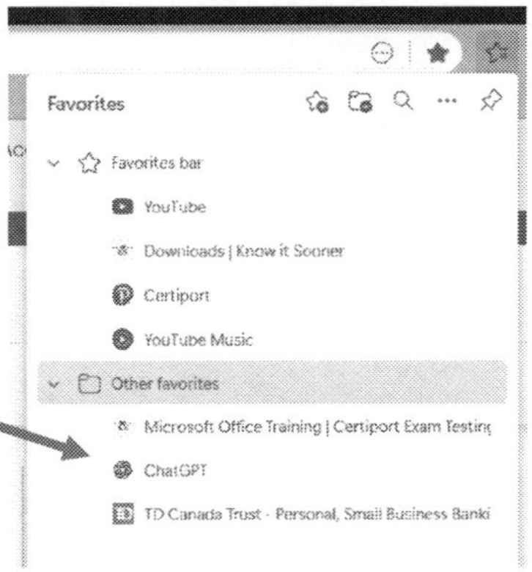

File Management

Terminology

Drives

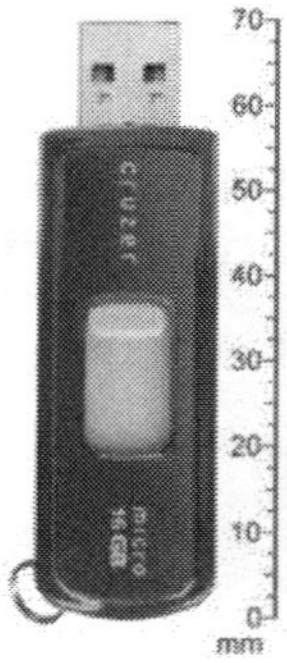

A drive is a physical piece of equipment where things are stored. The most popular is the hard drive that you cannot see, as it is normally inside the computer. It is typically referred to as Drive C. You can also have small drives that plug into a USB port on the computer (the rectangular slot). These are also called jump drives, thumb drives, memory stick, flash drive and USB stick. These will be referred to Drive D or a later letter.

Folders

Folders are created on drives for you to organize your documents and pictures and things like that. Think of a folder called Letters, and then all the letters you have written are stored inside of the Letters folder.
There is a folder called "My Documents" where all the Microsoft Office programs like to store things unless you tell it differently.

Files

Files can be pictures, documents (letters, reports, things that are created with a word processor like Microsoft Word), emails, spreadsheets and music. It might make sense to put similar file types into a folder or you might organize by project or job.

- 🗀 My Documents
    - 🗀 Finances
        - 🗀 Banking
        - 🗀 Budgeting
            - 🗀 2025
            - 🗀 2024
        - 🗀 Taxes
            - 2024
            - 2023
    - 🗀 Letters
        - 🗀 Cover Letters
        - 🗀 Misc Letters
        - 🗀 Recommendation Letters
    - 🗀 Pictures
        - 🗀 Holidays
            - 🗀 Camping
                - 🗀 Meadow Lake SK
                - 🗀 Slave Lake
            - 🗀 Vancouver
            - 🗀 Victoria

Creating your Filing System

1. Click on the yellow folder on your task bar at the bottom of your screen that says File Explorer when you rest your mouse on it.

2. Click on the folder or the drive you want to work with. If you have Office 365, you like have a OneDrive folder where you will work so that it is always backed up and easy to share. You can even access it from another device like your phone if it is stored in there.

3. You may see either a › sign or ⌄ a beside each folder. If you click on it, it will expand or collapse the existing folders.

   Clicking on the yellow folder will display the contents on the right side.

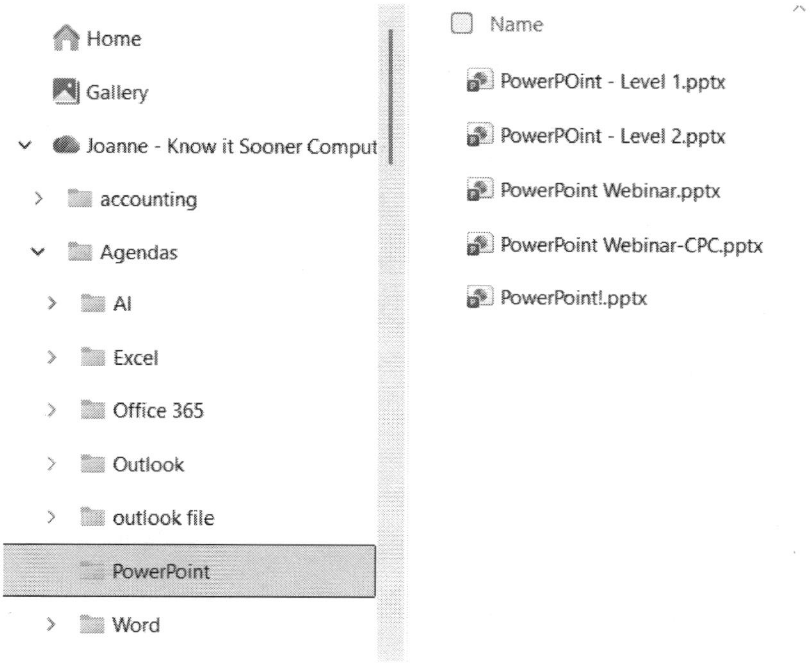

4. To create an additional folder, click on the yellow folder and then look for the New Folder command. The New Folder Command will likely be in a menu at the top of the screen or on the toolbar, depending on which version of Windows you have. It is usually available with a right mouse click as well.

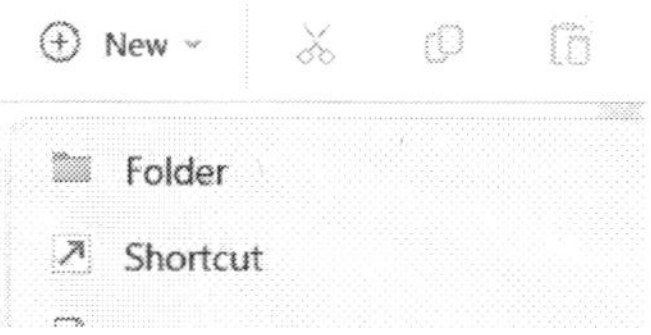

5. Type a name for the folder and press ENTER.

Moving your Documents

If you wish to move a document from one place to another, there are several ways to do that. One is to use the Windows Explorer. You will use the same window as you used to create the folder.

1. Click on the File Explorer program (yellow folder on your taskbar).
2. Navigate to the folder that you want to move your documents from.
3. Select the documents you want to move.
4. On the left side of your screen, use the scroll bar to find the folder you want to move it to. DO NOT CLICK ON IT!
5. Once you can see the folder, drag the documents you have selected over to the folder and drop them in!

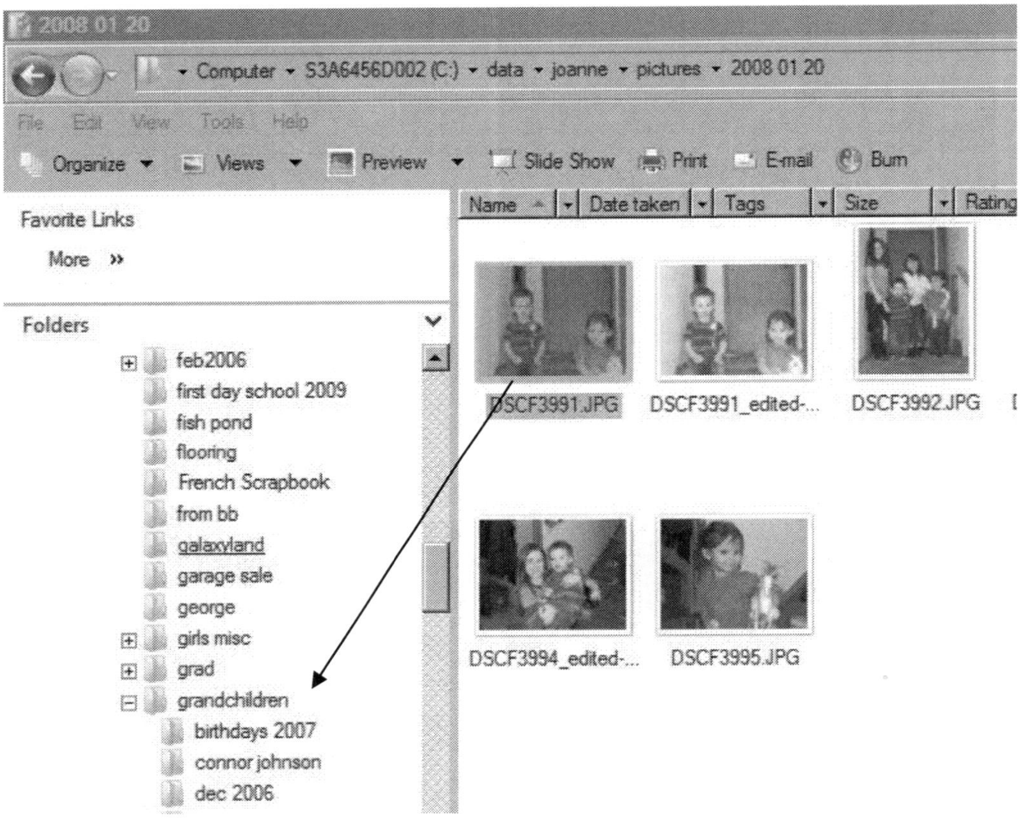

Selecting more than one document

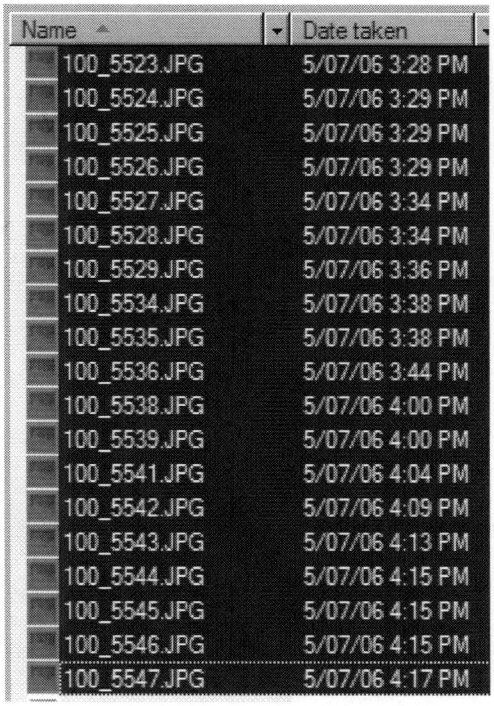

If they are adjacent to one another:

1. Click on the first one.
2. Hold the SHIFT key down and then click on the last one.
3. This selects all the ones in between. You can then click on any one of them and drag them, or you can press the DEL key and delete them!

If they are not adjacent to one another:

1. Click on the first one.
2. Hold the CTRL key down and click on the next one.
3. Keep the CTRL key held down while you click on all the others you want selected.
4. When you're done, release the CTRL key and move or delete them!

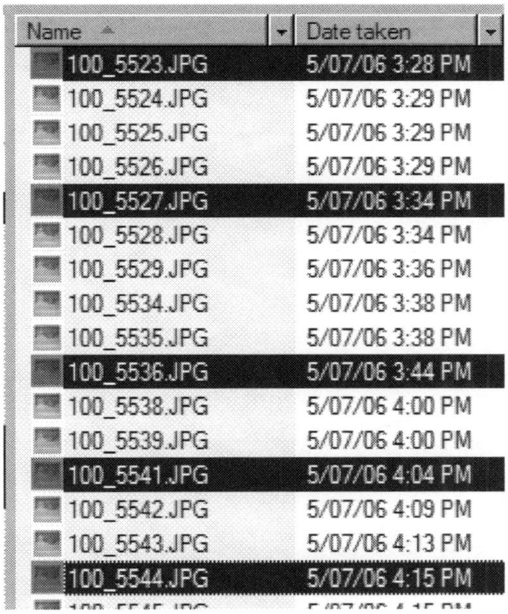

Save vs. Save As

When you are typing a document, you will want to save your changes. You need to name the document and give it a location to be stored in. There are two choices: Save and Save As. The first time you save a document, it doesn't matter which option you choose, you will get the Save As screen.

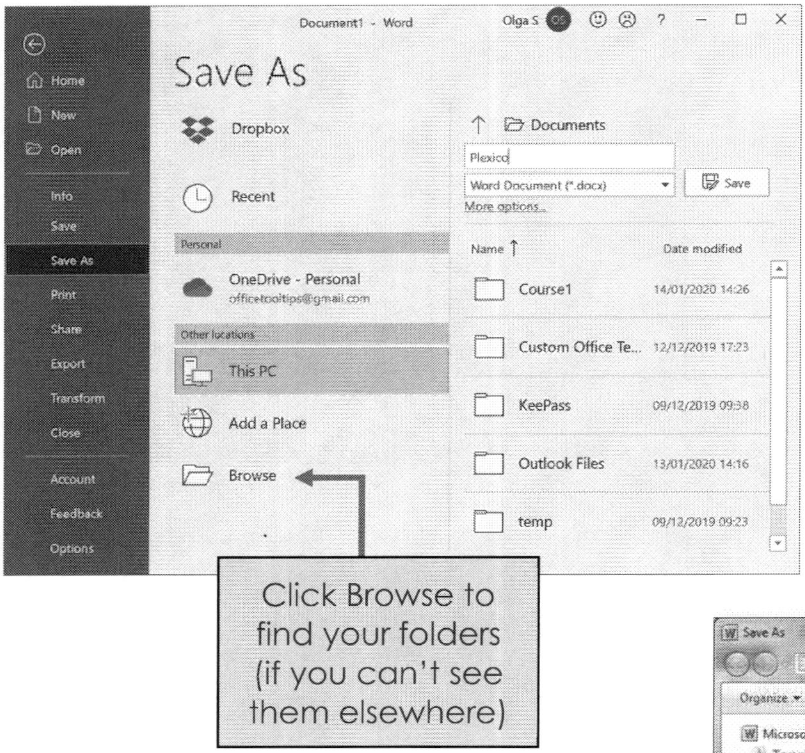

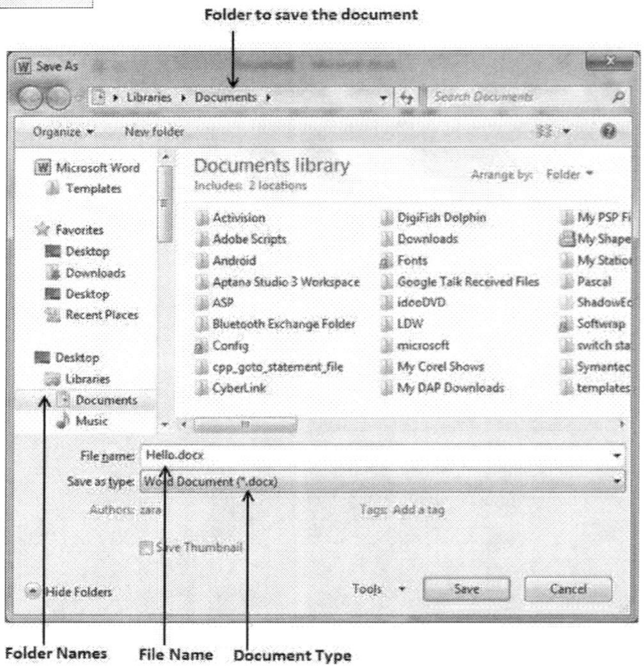

You will need to tell it where to save it to, the File Name, and what type of document you want it to be (often you can go with whatever it is suggesting).

Once you tell it this, the next time, you only need to click on Save and it will update the existing document and you will not have to tell it these choices again, unless you want to copy it and give it a new name.

Copy and Paste

This is one of the most useful, universal commands you will do on your computer! Who likes to retype information? I don't think anybody does. Copy and Paste allows up to take something from one program and use it in another. For example, if you had a paragraph in a letter in Microsoft Word that you wanted to put into an email, you would copy it from Word, and paste it into your email.

The steps are below. There may be variations of the procedures depending on which program you are working with.

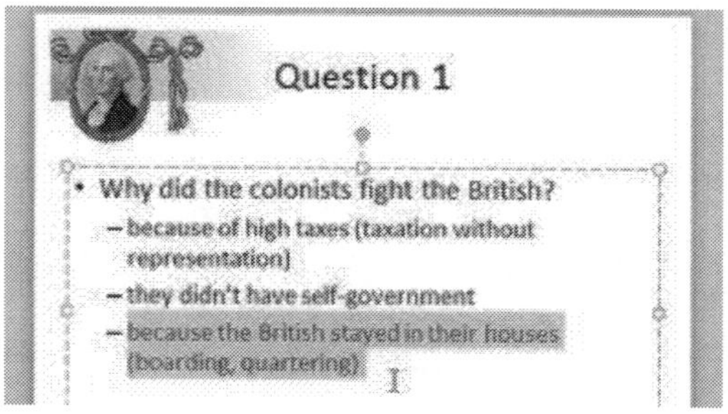

1. Select what you want to copy. Most of the time, do this by dragging your mouse over the text. If it's a picture or an icon you are copying, you don't normally need to do this step.

2. Next, you will perform the Copy command. This can be done several ways.
   - Click on the COPY button on your toolbar (if you have one)

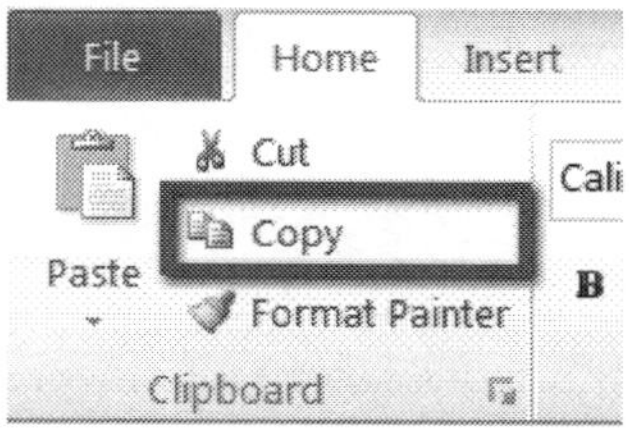

OR

   - Right Click on the selection and choose Copy.

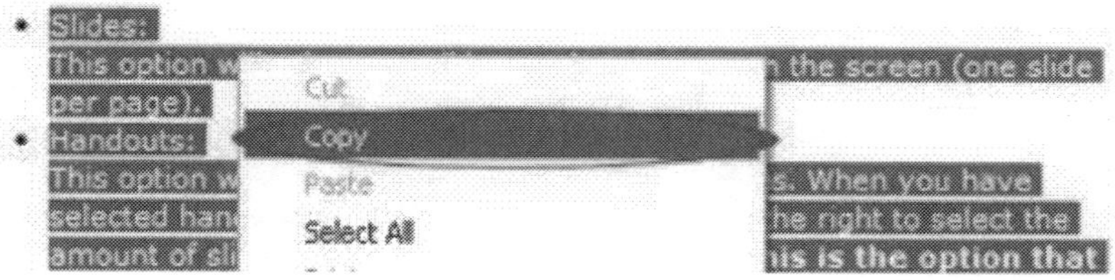

OR

   - Hold down the CTRL key and press C.

3. Now you need to go to the program where you would like to put the new text. Once you're there, you need to position your cursor exactly where you would like it to go.

4. You are now ready to Paste the information into the new location. Again, there are several ways to do this.

- Click on the Paste button, if you have one.

OR

- Right click and choose Paste.

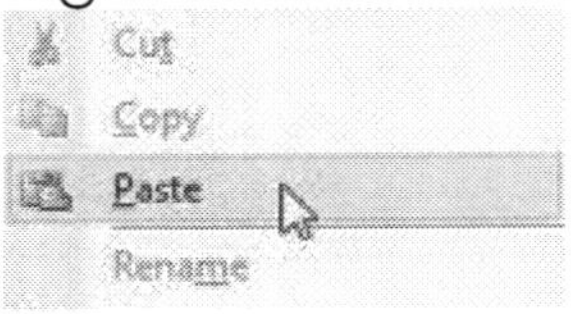

OR

- Hold down the CTRL key and press V.

Email

Getting Started

1. To send and receive email messages, you will need to start a browser program – either:
    - Internet Explorer
    - Microsoft Edge
    - Google Chrome

2. Go to the top of your screen and click once where you see an internet address like www.google.ca or something like that.

3. Type in the website that you can access your email from. It will likely be the same as the information at the end of your email address. For example, if my address is joanne@outlook.com, I would access it through outlook.com.

    Common email websites are:

    - hotmail.com
    - gmail.com
    - outlook.com
    - icloud.com
    - telus.com
    - shaw.ca
    - live.ca

- Click where it asks for your ID or user name and type your email address in full. There are never any spaces and it doesn't matter if you use upper or lower case. Keep it simple – use lower case.

4. Click where is says Password and type your password. Press ENTER or click on the Sign In button.

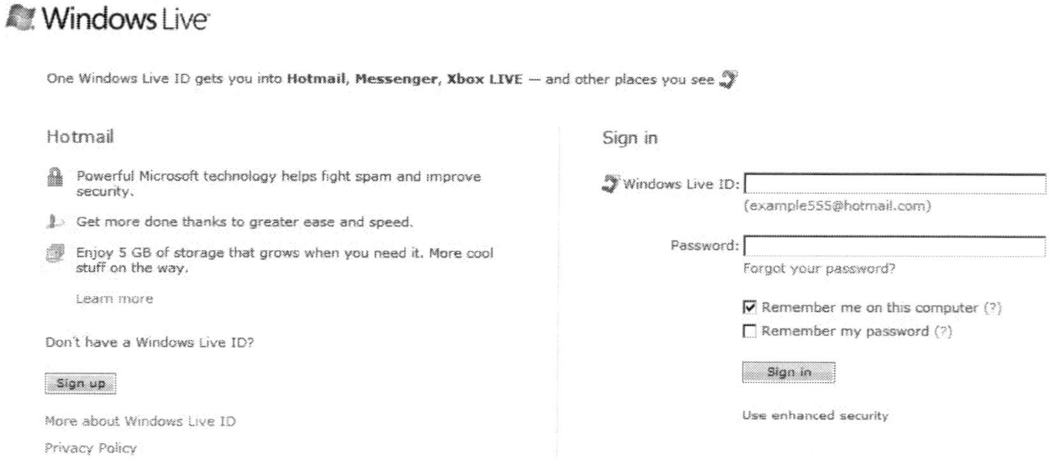

5. If you want to send an email, click on **New** or **Compose**. Some programs use a symbol rather than a written command.

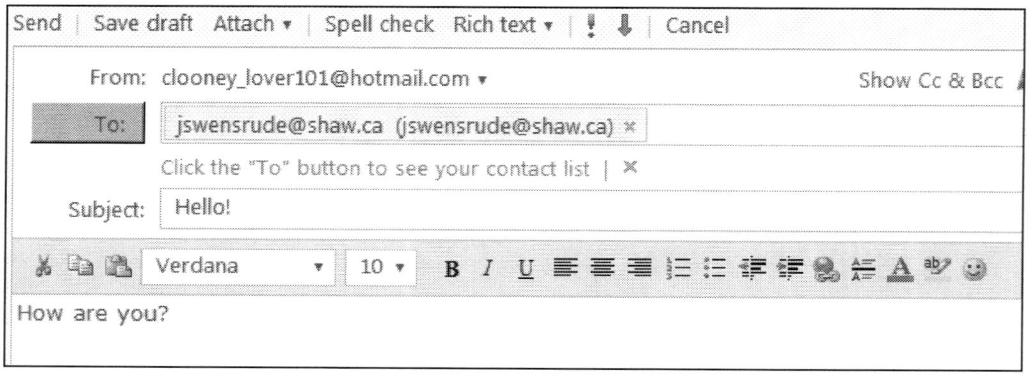

6. Type in the email address, the subject and your message. Press the Send button when you're done!

You may find that when you start typing, the email address or name of the person you're sending to automatically comes up if you have sent or received email from this person previously.

7. To read a message, click on the message line. You can then Reply to the sender or Forward it to someone else.

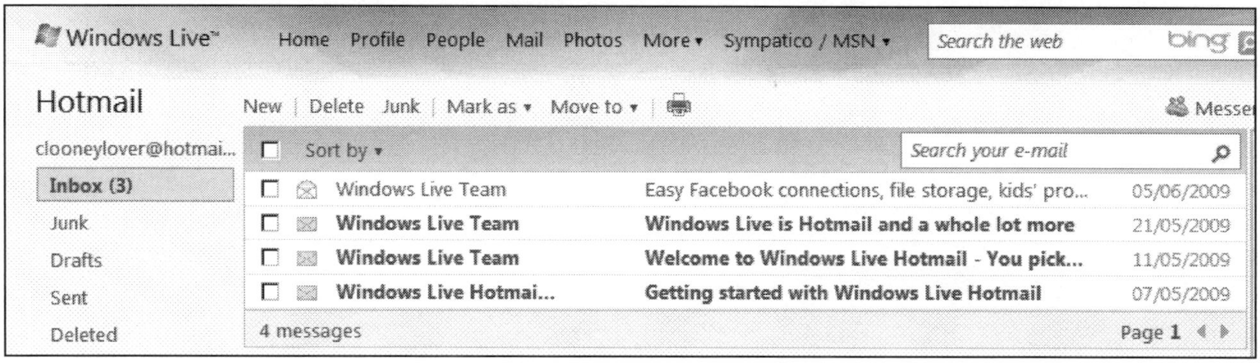

8. When you no longer want the email, simply click on the Delete button when you have selected your email, either while you are reading the email or when you are looking at the list of them (click on the check box first to select the email, then click on Delete).

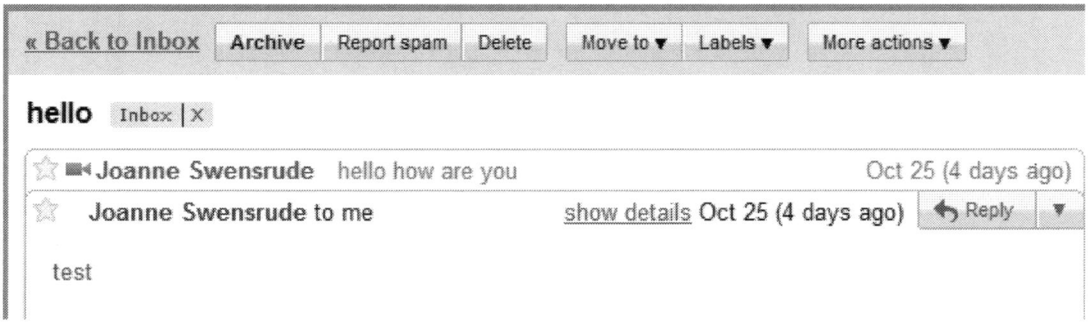

9. It then goes into your "Trash" folder. Some email programs empty the trash folder every 30 days. If you want to retrieve it or remove it, you must display the Trash folder first.

You click on it if you see it on the left side of the screen. If you don't, you may have to click on "More" and then it will display it.

Once you find your email in the trash, you can select it and then click the "Move to" button at the top and move it back to your inbox.

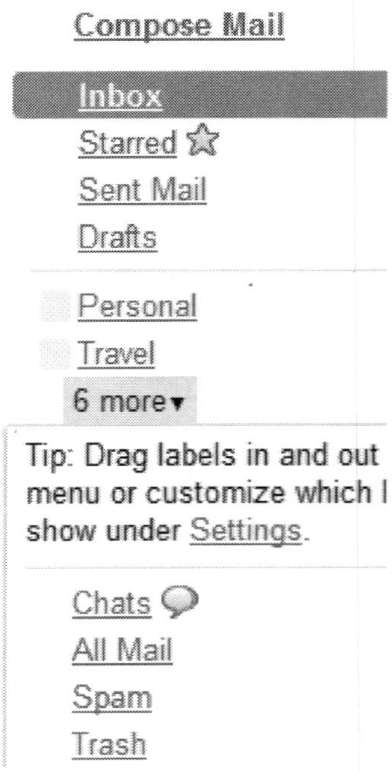

My Email Website:	
My Email Address:	
My Email Password:	

Attaching a Document to an Email

There may be times when a message alone is not enough. You may need to attach a word processing or spreadsheet file to the message so that you can reference a point within the file or ask someone to update a file which you have started. This allows the recipient to view and modify (if necessary) complex documents.
Although you can attach items such as photos, video and other objects, attaching an actual program can get tricky. Many times, programs attached to messages will not even be accessible to the recipient due to virus protectors and other security measures.

To attach a file object to a message, follow the steps below:

1. In a new email message, select the **Attach File** tool (usually located at the top of the screen) or a Paperclip button.

A box similar to the one below will be displayed. Some programs will have a screen that lists other choices but always watch for options such as "Browse" or "Choose from a List."

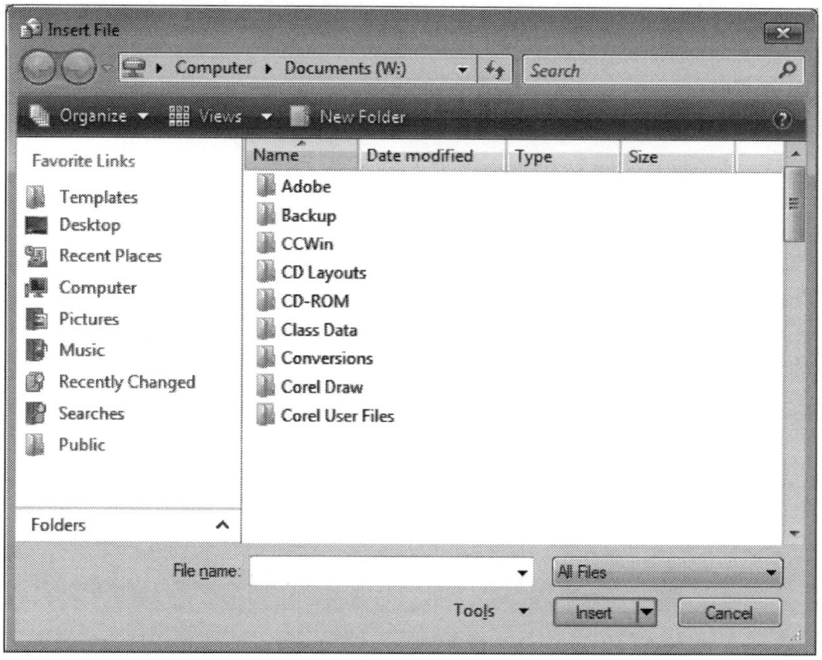

2. From the dialog box, find and select the file to be attached to the current message and click on 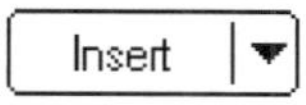. It may also say Open or Select.

The 10 Commandments of E-Mail Etiquette

Reprinted with permission from the etiquette page http://etiquettepage.com

In today's hurried culture, e-mail can seem like a quick way to communicate your message, but if you don't take the time to follow the basics, you might end up shooting yourself in the foot (in a business sense, of course). One misconstrued message, sent via iPhone while running from one meeting to another could affect a business relationship.

Here a few reminders to help you keep your digital communication etiquette in check:

1. **Thou shall use e-mail to convey only ideas and factual or logistical information, not emotions.** To express emotions and sentiment, take time for a one-on-one meeting or telephone conversation rather than sending an e-mail. The sound, tone, timber, and quality of your voice will help to better communicate your message and avoid misunderstandings.

2. **Thou shall write the topic of your message on the reference or subject line.** Always write a succinct, accurate description of what recipients can expect in the body of your e- mail in the subject line. It helps them prioritize their messages and quickly sort them for future reference. It also allows them to easily follow the trail of responses back and forth. If you correspond with the same people on multiple subjects, separate the e- mails by the appropriate topic clearly stated in the reference line.

3. **Thou shall address the e-mail using the name of the intended person.** Have you ever received a personal e-mail note destined for someone else? I did—and it was a love note that made me blush! I read half of it and realized it wasn't meant for me. Since then, I'm never sure I'm the intended recipient unless I see my name at the top.

4. **Thou shall use "blind copy" for e-mails sent to groups.** Avoid sharing names of the whole group via e-mail unless it's a small, closed group such as a Board of Directors or a Club and you know members have previously been given the list of names and e-mail addresses. E-mail addresses should be kept private.

5. **Thou shall never ever forward a chain letter that states if you do or don't do something within a certain time, your life will forever be changed.** It's nice to create change for someone but not by using threats. If you really must send the letter to others, remove the threatening language. If you don't, you will be excommunicated from the hall of good manners.

6. **Thou shall use "delivery receipt notification" only when it's imperative that you know if the intended recipient received it.** Don't create a need to send any unnecessary e-mail by using this tool. It can annoy people.

7. **Thou shall use capitalization, upper and lower case, and proper punctuation in e-mails as in all other written communications.** Studies have proven that if people read text written in all capital or all lower case letters, it takes much longer to read and understand a message. Use a standard way of writing.

8. **Thou shall close your e-mail message with heartfelt words that show that the sender is fully present.** Don't just rely on your automated signature line to close your e-mail. Let your recipients know that, indeed, a real person is sending them a message.

9. **Thou shall proofread your e-mail messages before sending them**. Although e-mail can be an informal way to communicate with people, it's always a good habit to use spell-check and read through your note before hitting "send" so that the message is clear. Sometimes just one missing word can make a difference. "I love your work," and "I loathe your work," clearly mean two very different things.

10. **Thou shall respond to e-mails within 24 hours.** Even if you cannot yet provide an answer, replying to someone's e-mail within a day lets the sender knows you received it. Sending immediate responses also keeps you organized and up to date on your e- mail correspondence.

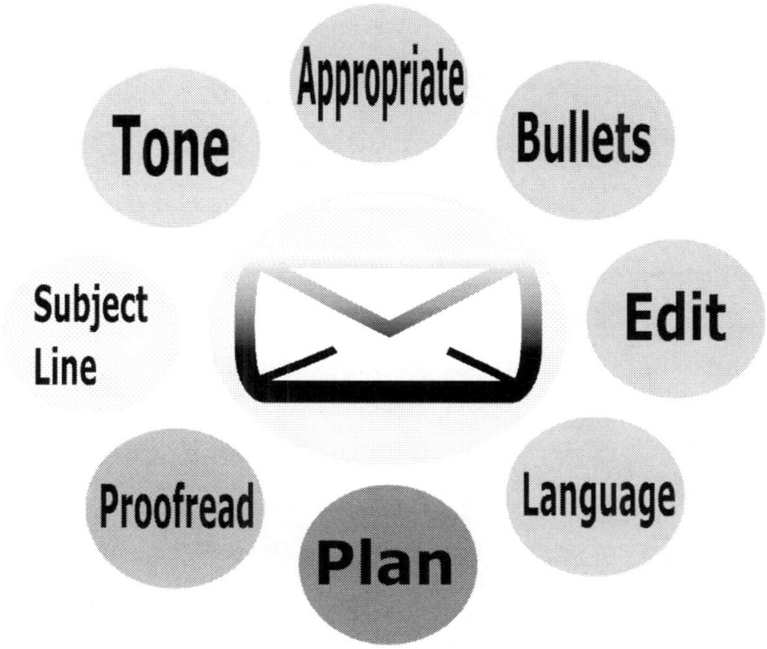

Outlook Tips

Finding Messages

Sorting

To quickly sort the messages by any one of the columns, simply click on the desired column heading and the messages will be sorted in that order. A small triangle is displayed in the currently sorted column. By default, the "From" and "Subject" columns are sorted in ascending sequence (A-Z) while the "Received" column is sorted in descending order.

There may be times when working with Outlook that you will need to reverse the order of the sort. You can quickly switch the sort order by clicking the column heading a second time.

If you sort by a text field such as FROM or SUBJECT, then you will be able to just start typing what you're looking for and it will take you to that place in your list of emails. For examples, if you were looking for all emails from "JOANNE", then sort by FROM and then just start typing JOANNE and you will see that it will take you to the first email from JOANNE.

Searching

To locate a message stored within Outlook, use the Search feature:

1. Click in the box located above the column headers of the Inbox.

   Your version of Outlook may display a slightly different search box but has similar options.

2. Enter the keyword(s) you are searching for. As you begin typing, Outlook will immediately start searching for messages based on what you are typing.
   Notice a new ribbon appears for more advanced search requests:

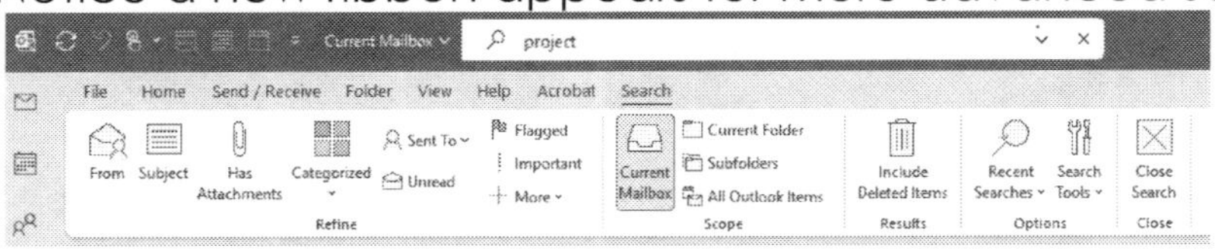

If you want to perform a more detailed search, use this ribbon to fine tune what you want to look for.

Find Related Items

If you are in an email and you'd like to see other emails either in this conversation (with the same subject line) or from the sender, then you can click on the Related button. It will list all the emails that you asked to see.

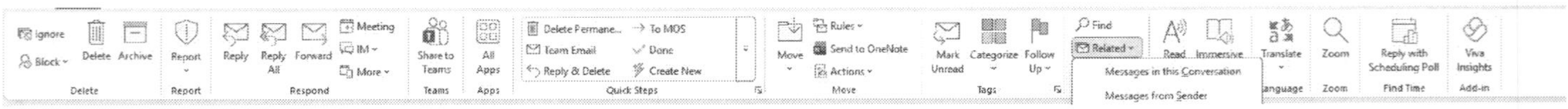

Managing your Inbox

If you would like to keep your Inbox clean, we suggest to do at least one of the 4 D's with every email.

- *Do it!*
- *Delegate it!*
- *Date it!*
- *Delete it!*

Do it!

If you deal with your email immediately, then delete it or file it in a folder for easy reference later. You may need to create a folder.

Creating a Folder

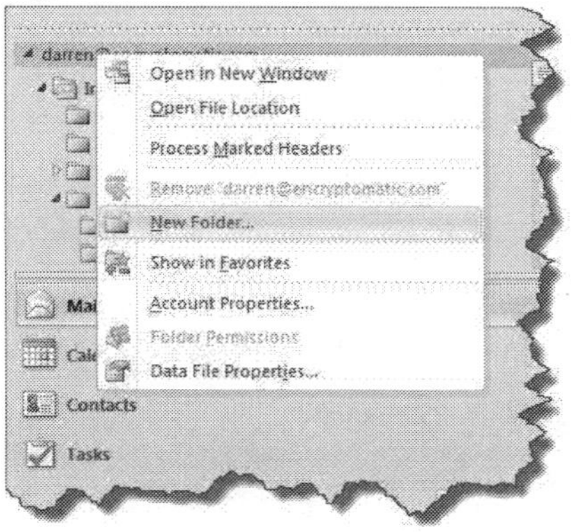

Simply Right click on the left hand side of the mailbox where you want your folder to appear. It is suggested to create a main folder first, then create subfolders inside.

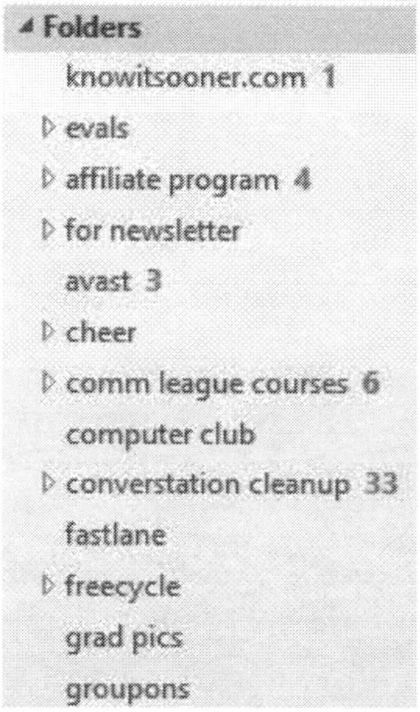

If you would like quick access to it, right click on it and you can add it to your favorites so it will appear at the top of your mailbox.

Move it to a Folder without Dragging it

You can see a list of your most recent folders by clicking on the Move button. This button is available from the main ribbon as well as by Right clicking on the message. You can access all your folders or create a new folder by choosing Other Folder.

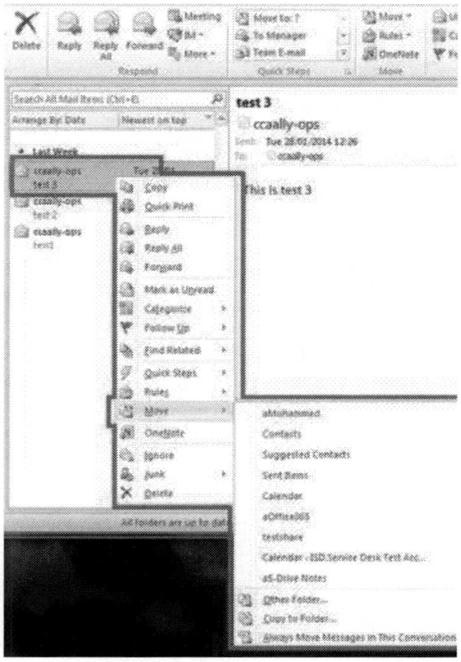

Delegate It!

If you forward an email to someone, you can simply just hit the Forward button and it prompts you to enter the recipient's name.

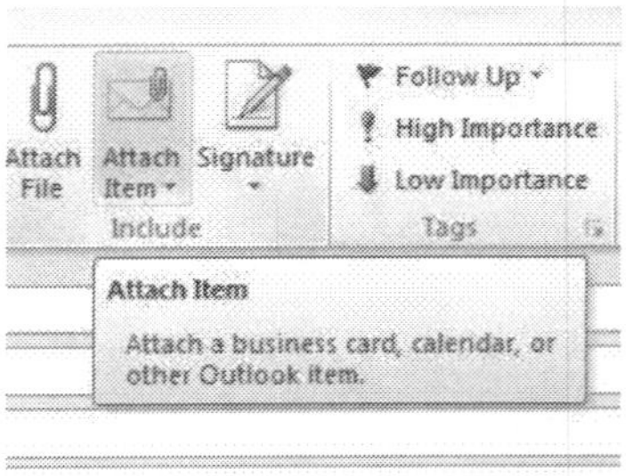

If you have several items to forward, look for the Attach Item button and you will be able to include several emails. Use the CTRL key to select more than one.

Depending on your version, the Attach Item command may be in the Attach File dropdown list.

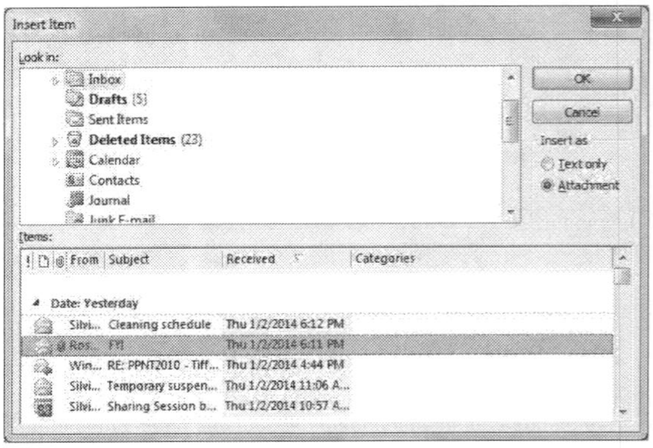

Date It!

Flagging Messages

If you want to flag a message for follow-up within a specific number of days, Outlook provides several predefined flags from which to choose. For example, you can add an instruction to call, reply or follow up on the message you are sending or receiving.

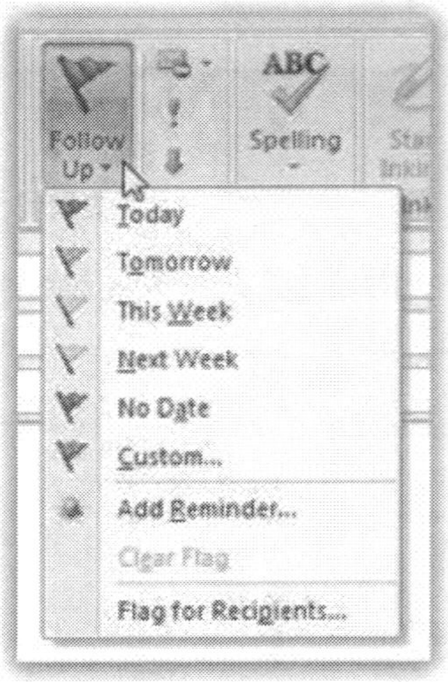

1. Click on the Follow Up tool (located within the Tags section on the Message ribbon) to set a flag for the current message. A pull-down list of options will be provided:

If you select **Custom** OR **Add Reminder** you will be taken to a dialog box where you can then choose what type of follow-up you are creating (call, forward, read, reply, etc.). This will show up with your tasks and if you set a reminder, it will come up with a reminder box at that time if you have Outlook open.

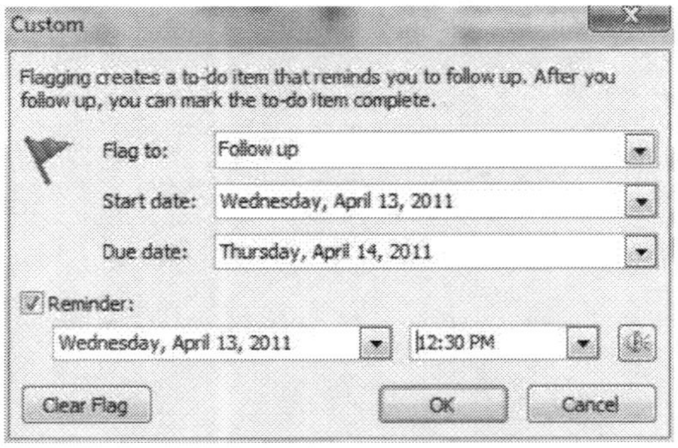

Delete It!

The traditional way to delete it to use the Delete key or click on the Delete button on the Ribbon. This puts it into the Deleted Items in case you need to retrieve it later.

If you know for sure you will not need to retrieve it, you can use the SHIFT DEL key combination to completely bypass the Deleted Items folder. This saves time storage and time later deleting it. You will be asked to confirm your action but you will NOT be able to retrieve it later so have caution using the feature.

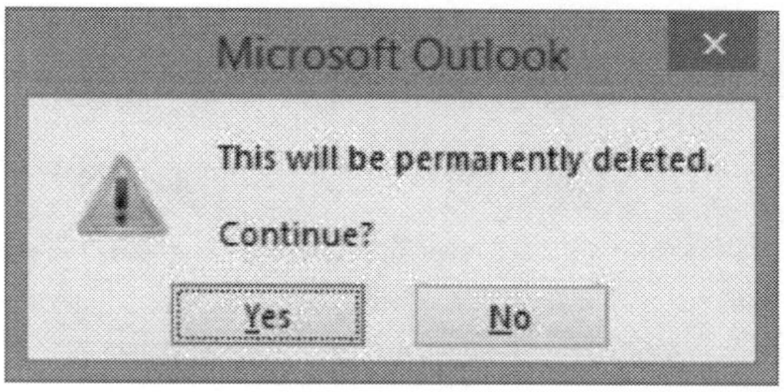

Conversation view

You may move your emails into different folders as you read and respond to them within your mail folders. Conversation view allows you to keep a track of any ongoing conversations (Replies and replies to replies etc.) irrespective of where you place them and a track is kept of where they were moved to. To turn this feature on tick the SHOW AS CONVERSATIONS box in the CONVERSATIONS group of the View Ribbon tab.

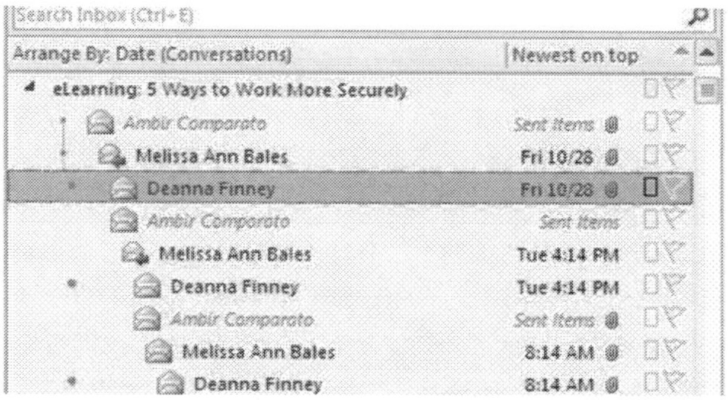

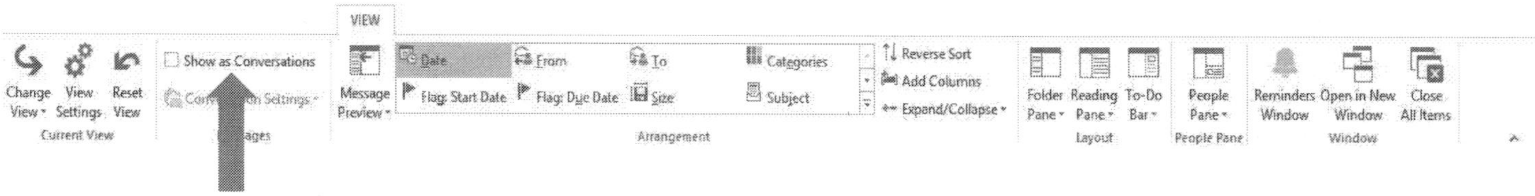

Dragging Items to Folders

In addition to dragging an email to a folder you've created (File, New Folder), you are able to create different types of Outlook items by dragging the email message to a different kind of folder. In most cases, this copies the email into the destination folder so you still have the email to reply to or file or delete.

If you drag an email to:	**You will:**
Calendar	Create an Appointment
Tasks	Create a Task
Notes	Create a Note
Contacts	Create a Contact for the Sender and the Email contents goes into the notes section
Deleted Items	Delete the Email

Send It Again!

Sometimes you want to resend a message to the same person or even a different person or maybe you forgot to attach a file.

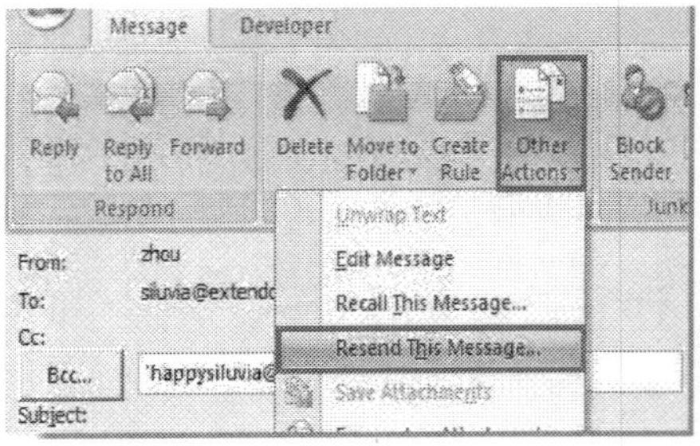

1. Find the message in your Sent Items folder.
2. Open the message.
3. Click the Actions menu.
4. Click Resend this message... A new message is created and can be altered before sending.

Automating Steps

Do you always want to move a message from a specific person or subject line to a folder?
Create a quick step or a rule.

Quick Steps

Quick steps are a fantastic feature that allows you to do regular things more easily within your mail folders. We will look at how to use them and create your own quick steps to make your use of Outlook quicker and easier. Quicksteps are like small macros (stored procedures) and only need a click to activate that procedure.

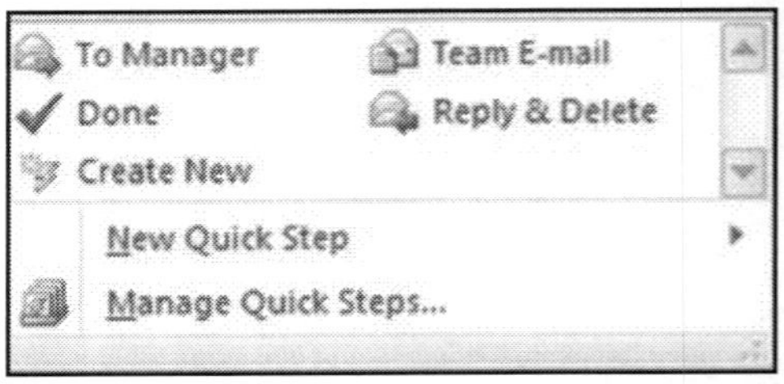

A number of quick steps have already been built into Outlook some you may use straight away and some you will have to edit.

1. To run a quick step, simply click on it on your toolbar.
   Depending on which quick step you choose, you may need to select a message first.

To create a quick step

Creating a quickstep needs you to think of time-consuming things that you wish could be done quicker and easier.

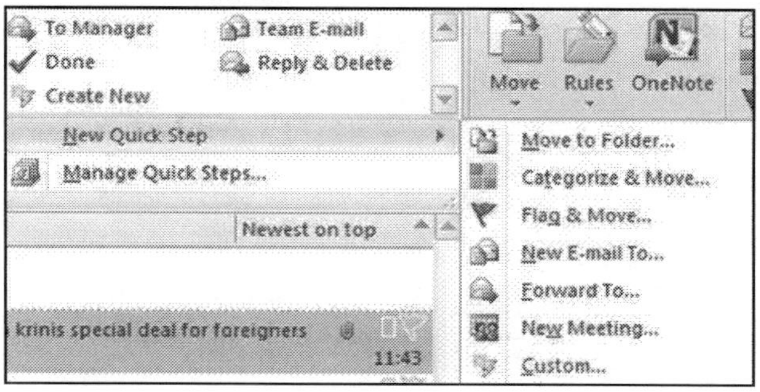

1. On the HOME ribbon in the QUICK STEPS group click on the down arrow to the right of the box to display all quick steps and further options
2. Click on CREATE NEW QUICK step
3. From the side bar that opens, choose what you would like to do
   We will create a new email to someone (or group)
4. Select NEW EMAIL TO… a dialog opens
5. Enter a name for the Quick step
6. In the TO box use the to button to select names from the address books
7. Click FINISH to create the Quick Step
8. The Quick Step will appear in the Quick Step menu. Click on it to run.

Rules

To quickly create a rule that automatically moves a message based on who it is from or who it is being sent to, follow the steps outlined below. You can also use the Subject line to determine where it should be filed.

1. Click on the Rules tool from the Home ribbon or from the main Outlook window within the message window.
2. Choose "Always Move Messages From" if you always want to move messages from a certain person. If you want to specify a specific subject line or specify other criteria, choose Create Rule…

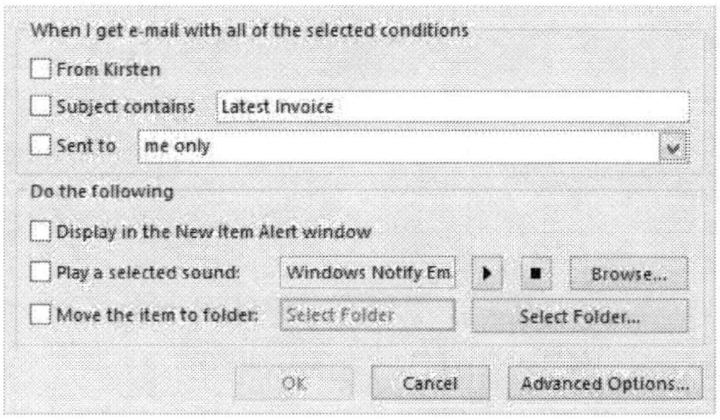

The following dialog box will be displayed. This dialog box is divided into two sections.

The top portion allows you to specify exactly which messages should be affected by the rule while the lower portion allows you to specify what action should be taken.

3. Check the appropriate boxes.
4. When done, click .

Working with Contacts

Adding Email Addresses to Contacts

On an incoming or outgoing email, right click on the person's email address and choose Add to Outlook Contacts. This creates a new contact record and allows you to enter additional information if desired.

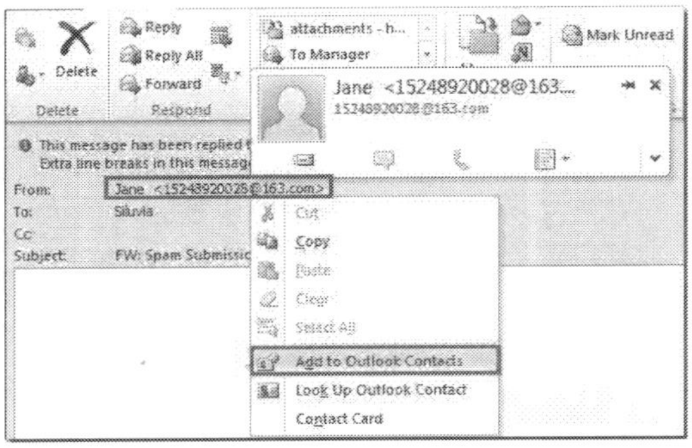

The Check Names Feature (CTRL K)

You DO NOT need to enter the full address or name of the recipient of your email message if they are in the global address book or your contacts if you are not on Exchange Server. Simply type part of their name and press CTRL or click the Check Names button on the toolbar to list any matches. If there is more than one match, it will list them, otherwise it will add the contact you specify to the address field you are on.

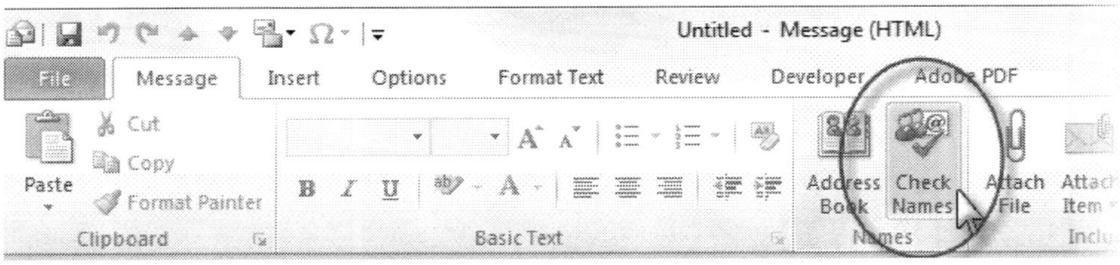

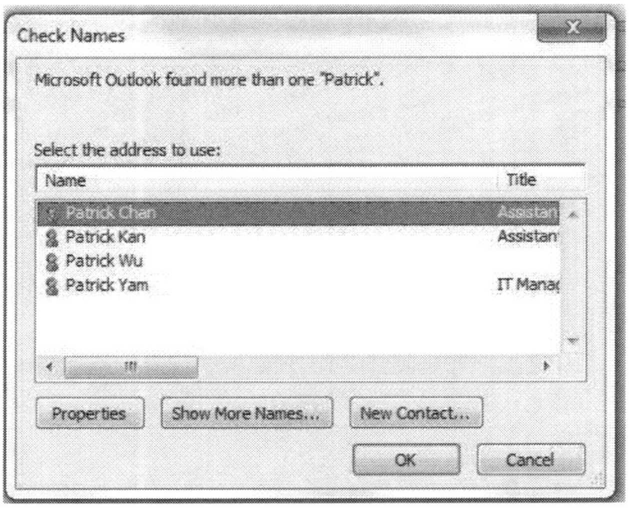

Calendar Tips

Viewing any Number of Consecutive Days

1. Go to Calendar and press ALT and the number of days you want to see. For example, press ALT **4** and Outlook will show you 4 days side by side.

View Non-Consecutive Days "Side by side"

1. On the calendar thumbnail on the left side, click on the first date that you want to see
2. Hold the CTRL key on the keyboard and then use the mouse to click on all the other dates that you are interested in.

Categorizing Meetings and Appointments in the Calendar

1. In the Calendar, right-click the meeting or appointment
2. Choose Categorize
3. Click a color category

To create a new category or change the name of a category

1. Choose All Categories...
2. Select the color you want to change and choose Rename OR
3. Choose New... to create a new category

Keep Meeting Invites in the Inbox

1. Choose File, Options, Mail
2. Scroll down to Send messages
3. Remove the checkmark ☑ Delete meeting requests and notifications from Inbox after responding

Miscellaneous Tips

Adding and Removing Outlook Favorites

1. Right-click the folder that you want to add to favorites
2. Choose Show in Favorites
3. Right-click the folder that you want to add to favorites
4. Choose Remove from Favorites

NOTE: Make sure that you remove folders from the Favorites rather than delete them. When you remove a folder from Favorites, the original folder in the folder list remains. Deleting a folder from Favorites deletes the folder and its contents from Outlook.

Creating a New Email, New Appointment, New Meeting, etc.

If you right click on the Outlook icon on the taskbar, a pop-up "jumplist" menu will appear. It will let you create an email message, appointment, meeting, contact, or task by selecting an item. Outlook doesn't need to be open when you click on an item, and the only part of the Outlook interface that opens is the part you need to perform the task you select.

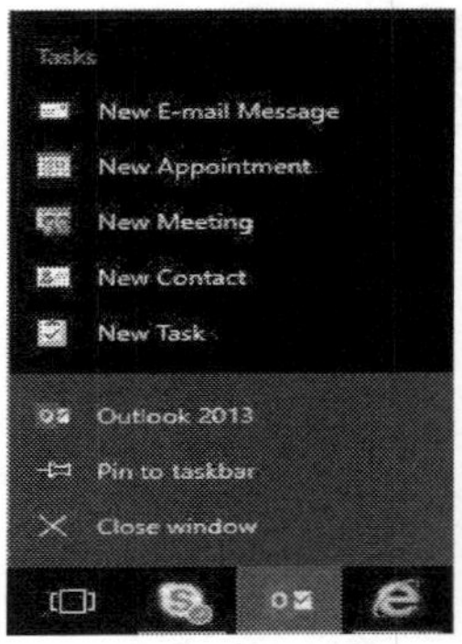

Auto-close Outlook's Message Window after a Reply

1. Choose File, Options, Mail
2. Scroll down to 

3. Add a checkmark next to 

Opening Multiple Windows

1. Right click on the (Mail, Calendar, People, Tasks) buttons on the bottom
2. Choose 

Now you will have a separate window for each item you choose. Great way to switch between the different areas within Outlook!

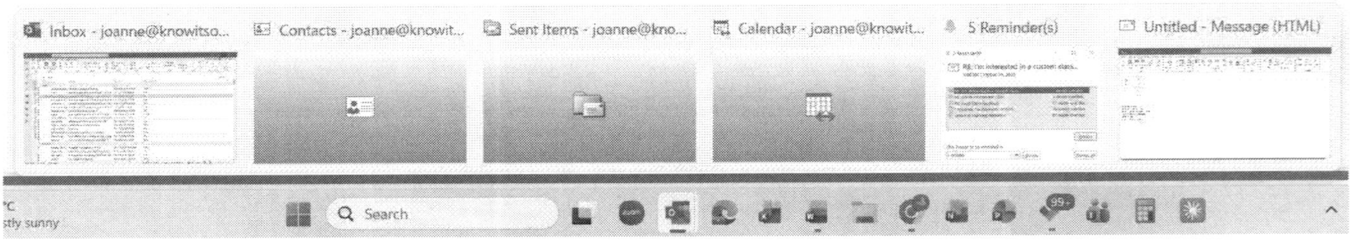

Insert a Screenshot in an Outlook Message

1. Create new mail message
2. Click in the body of the message
3. Choose Insert, Screenshot or Screen Clipping

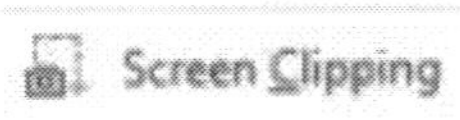

4. Choose from one of the existing open windows

   or Click and Drag around the part of the screen you'd like to capture.

   When you let go of the mouse, it will insert at the cursor's location.

Shortcut Keys

Press	**To create this item**
CTRL SHIFT A	Appointment
CTRL SHIFT C	Contact
CTRL SHIFT E	Folder
CTRL SHIFT L	Distribution list
CTRL SHIFT M	Message
CTRL SHIFT Q	Meeting request
CTRL SHIFT N	Note
CTRL SHIFT K	Task
CTRL SHIFT S	Post in this folder
Press	**To**
CTRL SHIFT	Switch to Inbox from another Outlook folder
ALT ENTER	Display message properties
CTRL A	Select All
CTRL SHIFT B	Open Address Book
CTRL C	Copy selected text
CTRL D or DEL	Delete selected message
CTRL E	Opens Search Dialog
CTRL F	Forward to selected message
CTRL SHIFT F	Open Message Search Dialog
CTRL N	Create new item (depends what folder you're in)
CTRL P	Print selected messages
CTRL R	Reply to the author of selected message
CTRL SHIFT R	Reply to author and all recipients of selected message.
CTRL U	Marks Message as Unread
CTRL <	Display previous message
CTRL >	Display next message
ESC	Close window

Introduction to Artificial Intelligence and ChatGPT

What is Artificial Intelligence?

Artificial Intelligence (AI) refers to computer systems that can perform tasks typically requiring human intelligence. These include understanding language, recognizing patterns, solving problems, and making decisions. Modern AI tools like ChatGPT use machine learning to understand your questions and provide helpful, conversational responses.

What is ChatGPT?

ChatGPT is a conversational AI assistant developed by OpenAI. Think of it as an intelligent assistant that can help you with writing, research, problem-solving, and learning new topics. You type questions or requests in plain English, and ChatGPT responds conversationally. It's available free at chat.openai.com, and you can also access other AI assistants like Claude (claude.ai), Microsoft Copilot, and Google Gemini.

Getting Started with ChatGPT

- Go to a browser and go to chatgpt.com and create a free account
- Type your question or request, also referred to as a prompt, in the message box at the bottom
- Press Enter or click the send button
- Review the response and ask follow-up questions as needed

Tips for Better Results

- **Be specific:** Instead of "Write an email," try "Write a professional email to a client explaining a project delay"
- **Provide context:** Share relevant background information to get more tailored responses
- **Ask for revisions:** If the first response isn't quite right, ask ChatGPT to modify it
- **Verify important information:** Always fact-check critical details, especially for technical or legal matters

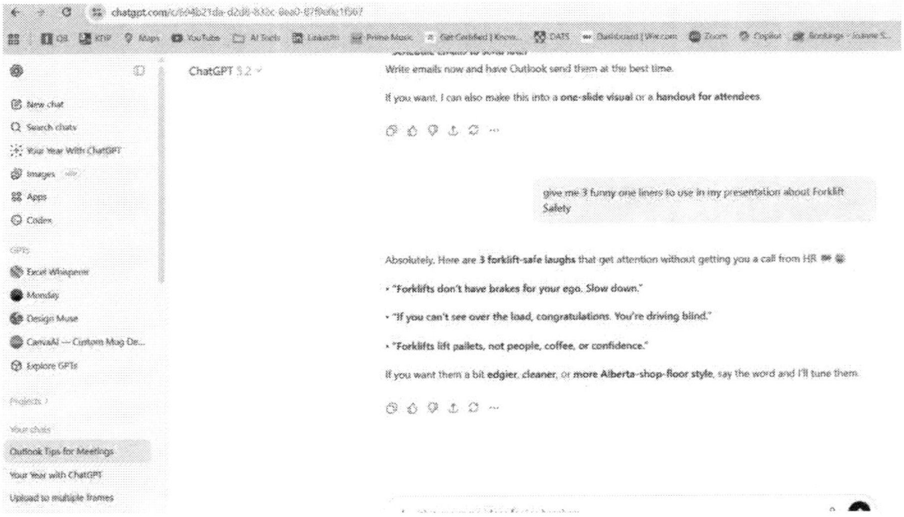

Practical Prompts to Try

Business Writing

- *"Draft a professional email requesting a meeting with my manager to discuss a project proposal"*
- *"Write a brief summary of our quarterly sales meeting for team members who couldn't attend"*
- *"Help me write a polite follow-up message to a client who hasn't responded to any of my emails"*
- *"Create an agenda for a one-hour team meeting about improving customer service"*

Document Creation

- *"Generate a template for tracking monthly expenses with categories for office supplies, utilities, and payroll"*
- *"Create a checklist for onboarding new employees at a small business"*
- *"Draft a brief company policy on remote work that covers working hours and communication expectations"*

Data Analysis & Organization

- *"Explain how to create a pivot table in Excel to analyze sales data by region"*
- *"Help me organize customer feedback into themes and suggest improvements"*
- *"Summarize this lengthy report and highlight the three most important takeaways"*

Job Search & Career Development

- *"Review my resume and suggest improvements for applying to project manager positions"*
- *"Write a cover letter for an administrative assistant position emphasizing my organizational skills"*
- *"Help me prepare for a job interview by generating common questions for a customer service role"*
- *"Suggest skills I should develop to advance my career in digital marketing"*

Learning & Skills Development

- *"Explain the basics of Excel formulas for someone who's never used them before"*
- *"Create a simple study plan to help me learn how to be a better public speaker in two weeks"*
- *"Break down the concept of cloud storage in simple terms for a technology beginner"*

Personal Organization

- *"Help me create a weekly schedule that balances work, exercise, and family time"*
- *"Suggest a simple system for organizing my digital files and folders on my computer"*
- *"Generate ideas for a family vacation in Alberta that includes outdoor activities"*

Creative & Fun Applications

- *"Write a funny birthday poem for my colleague who loves coffee and always arrives 5 minutes late"*
- *"Create a treasure hunt with 5 clues for my grandkids to find hidden treats around my house"*
- *"Suggest creative team-building activities for a small office that don't require leaving the building"*
- *"Help me plan a surprise retirement party including theme ideas, decorations, and a speech outline"*
- *"Generate 10 conversation starter questions for a family dinner to get everyone talking and laughing"*
- *"Create a personalized crossword puzzle using words related to my company's products and services"*
- *"Write a creative 'out of office' auto-reply message that's professional but has personality"*
- *"Help me create a fun weekly newsletter for my team with interesting facts and motivation"*
- *"Generate ideas for office pranks that are harmless and appropriate for April Fools' Day"*
- *"Create a recipe using only ingredients I have: chicken, rice, carrots, and soy sauce"*

AI tools like ChatGPT work best when you treat them as collaborative assistants. Don't hesitate to ask follow-up questions, request changes, or try different approaches. The more you practice, the better you'll become at crafting effective prompts. Most importantly, use AI to enhance your productivity while maintaining your own judgment and creativity in final decisions.

Have fun experimenting! The best way to learn is by trying different prompts and seeing what works. AI can be both a practical business tool and a creative partner for everyday tasks.

Microsoft Word

Downloading Documents from Our Website

There will be times in this course where you will be asked to download a document from our website so that you have some text to work with.

1. Using a browser such as Google Chrome, go to www.knowitsooner.com. You may want to make it a Bookmark/Favorite if you haven't already done so.
2. Click on Downloads. It's near the top of the screen.
3. Click on Word or Excel, depending on the program you are practising at the time.
4. When you find the document or spreadsheet, that you want, rest your mouse to the left of it.
5. Click the round dot to the left of the spreadsheet you want to download.
6. Click Download.
7. Click the round dot again to un-select it.

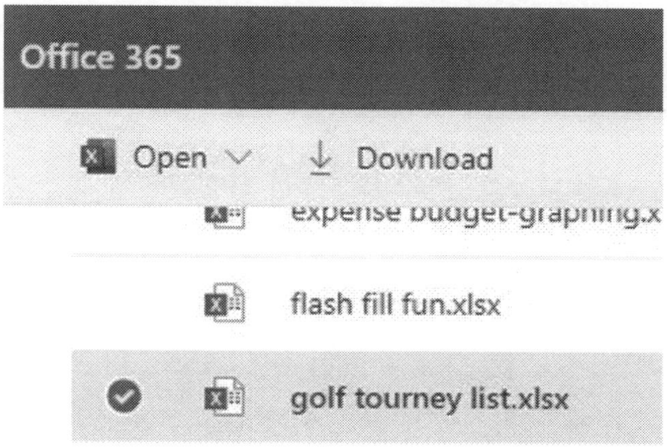

   It will then download it to your computer and will likely put it in the Downloads folder.

8. You will either see it on the top right corner of your screen or bottom left. Find it and click on it.
9. The program (ie. Word or Excel) will open the document you chose. There may be a bar at the top asking you to Enable Editing. Click on the button to be able to edit the document.
10. Click on File, then Save As to save this into your Documents folder so that you can open it up later. Remember to click on File Save in order to save all the enhancements, changes and typing that you have done.

The Word Screen

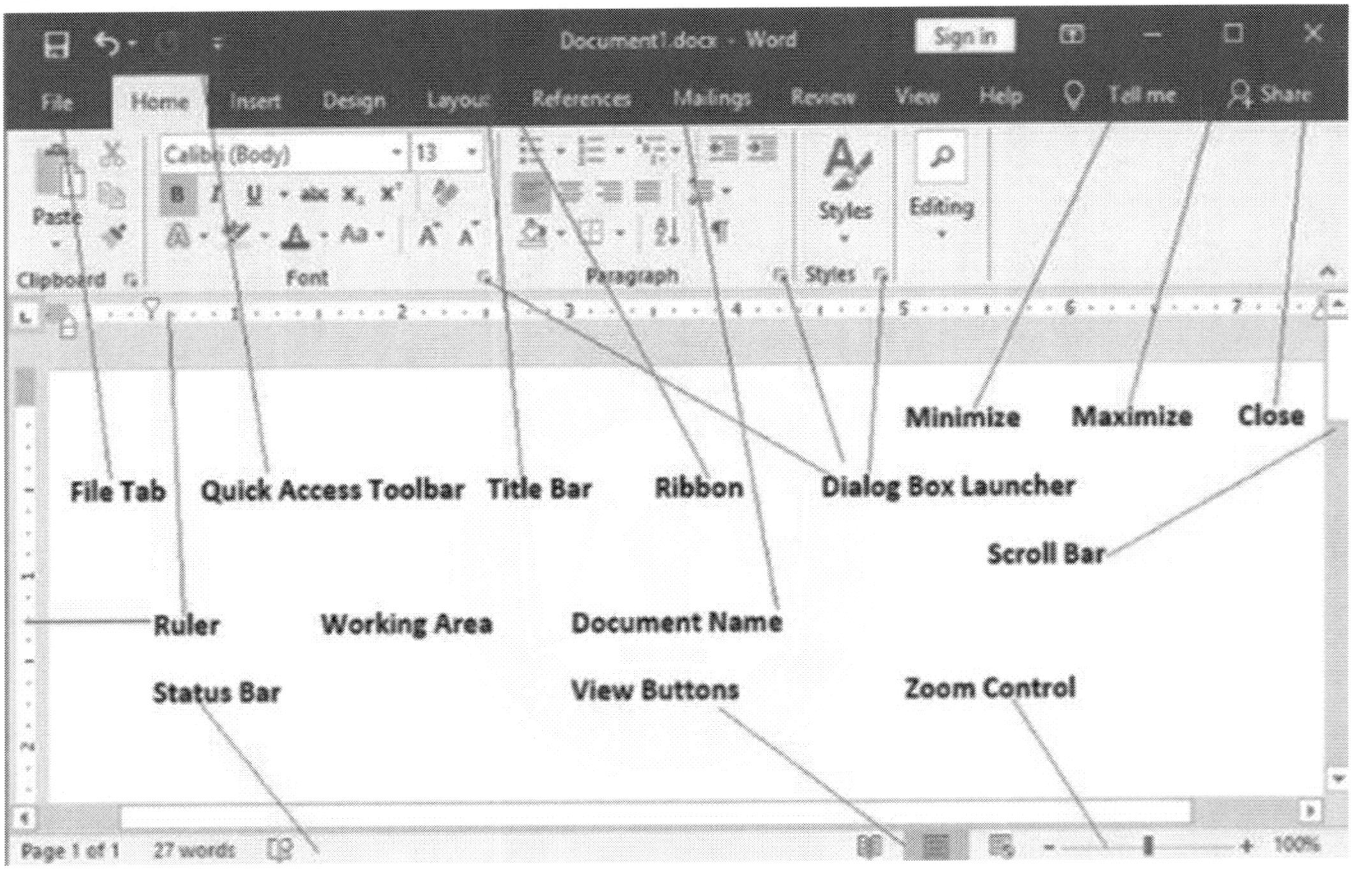

Quick Access Tool Bar Provide tools to access commonly used functions.

Close Button Used to close active window.

Ruler Shows the left and right indents and tab stops.

Ribbon This holds many tabs that hold time saving buttons. For example, the Page Layout tab contains commands relating to setting up your print job. If you double click on one of the ribbon tabs, the ribbon will be minimized in order for you to maximize your work space. Double click it again to bring it back to normal size.

Insertion Point Indicates the position of the cursor.

Status Bar Lists document information such as current page number. You can right-click on the status bar to get more options.

Zoom Tool This option allows you to zoom in and out to see more or less of your page. Click to plus button to zoom in or the minus to zoom out.

Quick Access Toolbar

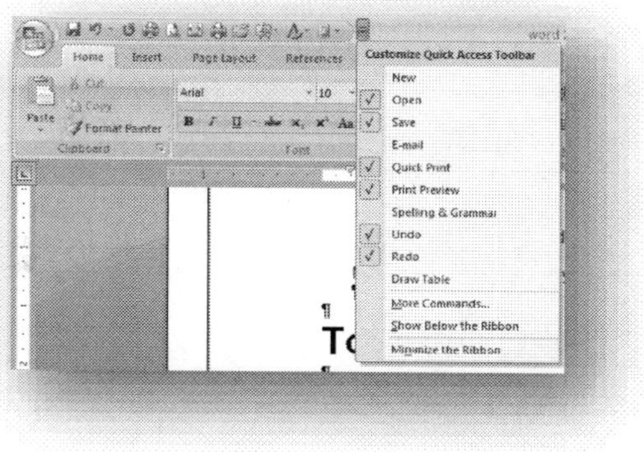

To customize the Quick Access Bar there are a couple methods.

1. Click on the arrow to the right of the Quick Access Bar.

2. This lists some popular choices. Choose one by clicking on it or click on Customize to see more choices.

3. If you choose More Commands, you will see plenty of categories that list available commands. You can double click on the button to make them show up on your quick access toolbar.

   You can also change the order of the buttons by clicking on the arrows to move the selected button around.

A quick way to add a button to your toolbar is to right click on it and choose Add to Quick Access Toolbar!

Viewing Your Document

1. Click on the plus or minus sign at the bottom right corner of your screen. This allows you to make your document larger on the screen.
2. Notice the four viewing buttons to the left of this Zoom bar. These toggle between Print Layout, Full Screen Reading Web, Outline and Draft view. Click on each of them to see how it displays your document.

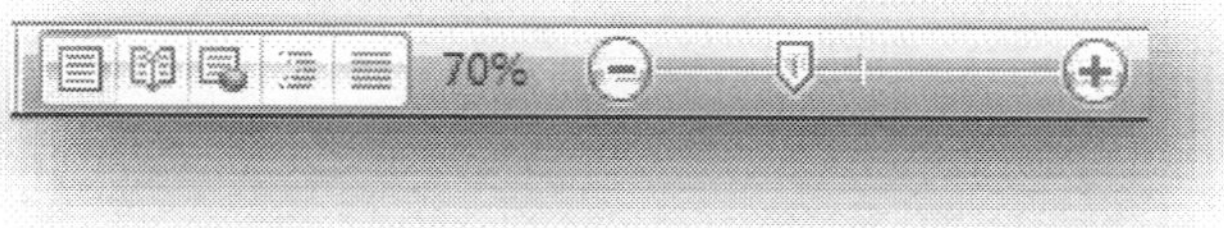

You can also hold the CTRL key and spin the wheel on your mouse to zoom in and out!

Status Bar

The default **Status Bar** displays the page number and the number of words in the document. You can right click on the status bar to select other information to display such as the section number of total number of pages.

Non Printing Characters

To assist in formatting your document, there are some special codes that tell you what key has been pressed (ie. Space, tab, enter, etc). You can turn this display on and off by clicking the Show/Hide button on the Home ribbon tab.

• (dot)	Space
→	Tab
¶	End of paragraph (created with ENTER)
↵	Line break (new line, same paragraph created with SHIFT ENTER)
-----Page Break-----	Hard Page break (created with CTRL ENTER)

Setting Defaults

You may want to make the following changes to your Word screen for maximum benefit.

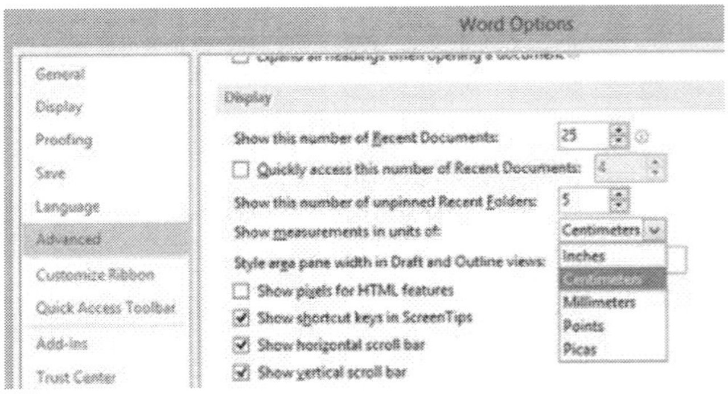

1. Turn on your ruler (View ribbon tab)
2. Change the measurement from Centimeters to Inches (File menu, Options, Advanced)

Working with Documents

Creating a Document

Word allows you to open and work on many documents in the same session. You can either pick from a list of templates or quickly create a blank document

Using the New Command from the File Menu

To see a list of templates to choose from, select New from the File menu. You will see a list of templates to choose from. You can also type in a search term. Here is just a few examples of documents you will see templates for:

- Letters
- Memos
- Calendars
- Fax cover sheets
- Certificates
- Invitations
- Greeting cards
- Flyers
- Business cards
- Many More

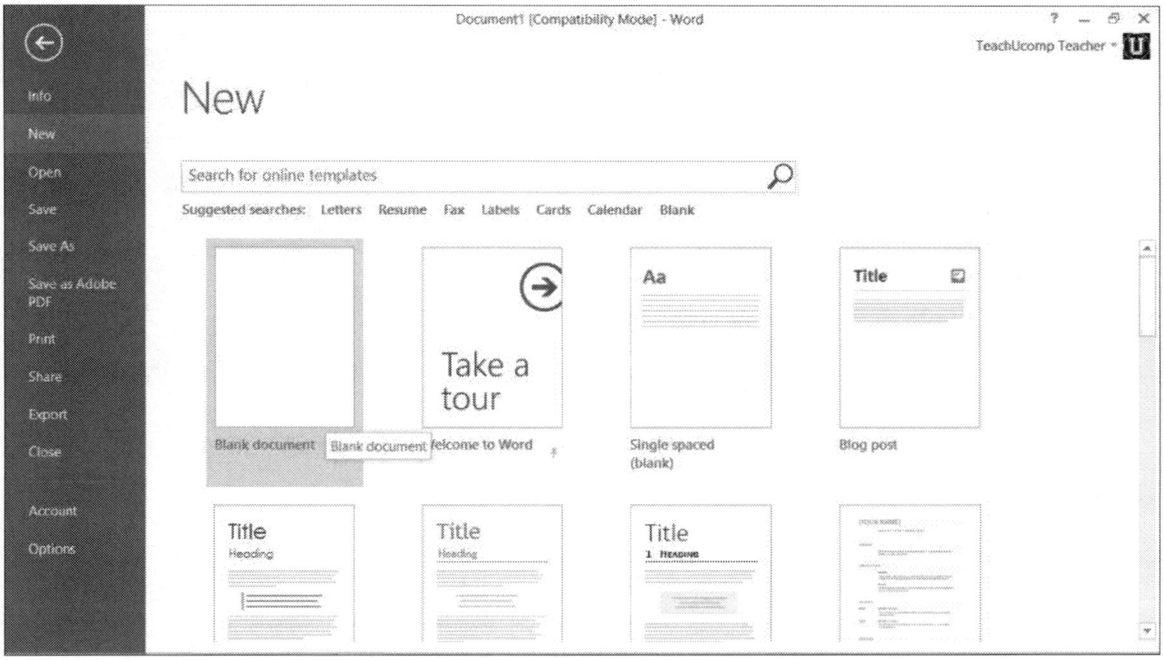

Quickly Create a Blank Document

Press CTRL N to create a new, blank document.

Opening a Document

When you want to edit a document that has already been stored on disk, you need to open a copy of the document (file) into a document window. Files are stored in directories or folders. The **Open** command allows you to see a list of what is in the current directory and also what files are in other directories. It will allow you to see the list for any directory that you have access to.

1. Choose Open from the File menu button or on your Quick Access toolbar if you have added it.
2. Click once on any document in the recently used file list or either Computer or Browse if your document is not listed. Choose from a recently used folder or the Browse button to list all folders.
3. Find your folder and double click to open it and when you see your document, click on it and then OK (or double click on the file name).
4. If it's a document that you frequently use, click on the pushpin to ensure it stays on the first screen you saw when you chose File Open.

Switching Between Documents

When you have more than one document open, look down at the bottom of your screen and click on the icon of the program you're in (ie. Word). You should see all open documents, even if you have minimized them.

Saving a Document

When you create/edit a document, any changes you make are stored temporarily in your computers active memory. A document is not stored permanently until you save it to a hard disk, network drive or memory stick.

There are at least three ways to save files in Word.

1. Choose **Save or Save As** from the File menu - does the same as Save on a brand new document but creates a new file on a file that already has a name.
2. Save on your toolbar- opens the Save As dialog box if it's never been saved before. Otherwise, it just updates the existing version.

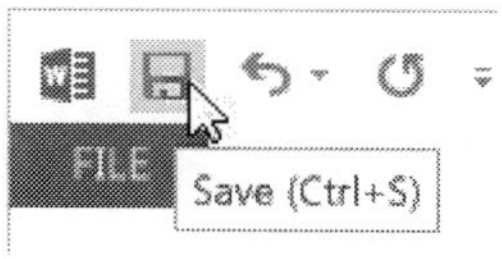

3. This can also be done by pressing CTRL S.

Note...if you open an old document saved in the previous version, it will automatically save back to that same version/format.

If you want to update it to the newest version, choose Word Document as the file type. Know that you may not be able to share this document with someone that doesn't have a newer version of Word or Google Docs, etc.

We typically save documents in the Documents folder or to your OneDrive space. You may create folders here to make it easier to find later.

Selecting and Editing

The select feature of Microsoft Word allows you to highlight or select text, tables or graphics. Once selected, you can then use the selection in combination with other features. In this module you will learn how to select text with both the mouse and the keyboard and then perform other functions with the selected text such as bolding, underlining, moving and copying.

1. SELECT
2. DO

In other words, if you don't select the text first, then the "Doing" will not DO much good! Microsoft Word always needs to know what text you want to affect by the command you are giving it.

Selecting Text – Mouse

WHEN THE CURSOR IS AN I-BEAM:

Click & Drag	Selects an undefined portion
Double Click	Selects a word
CTRL Click	Selects a sentence

WHEN THE CURSOR IS AN ARROW IN THE SELECTION BAR (very left side of screen):

Click	Selects the line
Click and Drag	Selects more than one line
Double Click	Selects a paragraph
Triple Click	Selects the whole document

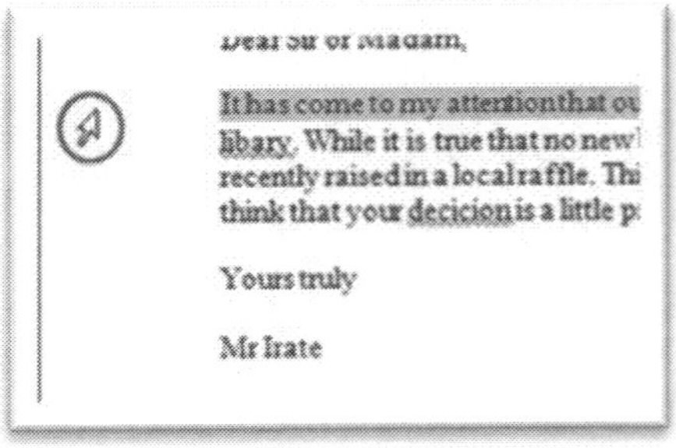

Selecting Text – Keyboard

SHIFT →	Selects right one character
SHIFT ←	Selects left one character
SHIFT ↑	Selects up one line
SHIFT ↓	Selects down one line
SHIFT END	Selects to end of line
SHIFT HOME	Selects to beginning of line
SHIFT CTRL →	Selects to the right one word
SHIFT CTRL ←	Selects to the left one word
SHIFT CTRL ↑	Selects up one paragraph
SHIFT CTRL ↓	Selects down one paragraph
SHIFT CTRL HOME	Selects to beginning of file
SHIFT CTRL END	Selects to end of file
CTRL A	Selects the whole document

Deleting Text

It is very simple to delete text you no longer need. If you don't have any text selected, you can choose to use the DEL key or the BACKSPACE key. The difference is which character you will be removing.

DEL key	removes the character to the right of the flashing cursor
BACKSPACE key	removes the character to the left of the flashing cursor

You can also select the text using the above methods and press the DEL key on your keyboard.

Undo

Occasionally you will delete or perform an action which you would like to take back. Microsoft Word allows you to make these corrections very effectively with Undo function.

UNDO REDO

This command is available on the Quick Access toolbar or by pressing CTRL Z. Click the curved arrow once to undo the last action. Click the underlined arrow next to it to see a list of commands you have performed and click on the desired command you wish to undo.

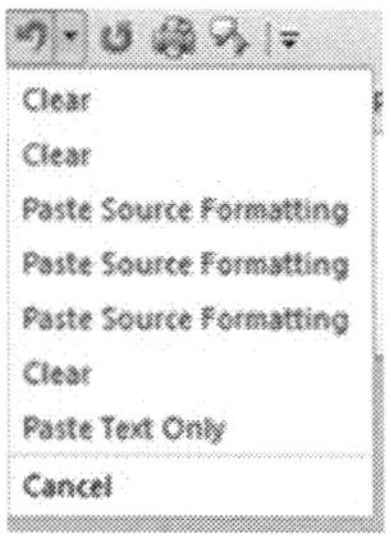

You can use Undo to reverse most actions such as typing or deleting text, inserting graphics, and changing formats such as tabs and margins.

Word will not let you Undo an action that did not affect the document such as scrolling.

When using Undo it is best to choose Undo immediately after the incorrect action has been performed.

Redo

If you undo something that you really shouldn't have undone, you are able to Redo it (this will UNDO YOUR UNDO!!).

Typing Replaces Selection

One feature in Word you can utilize is the Typing Replaces Selection command. Simply select the text you don't want and type the text you want to be there instead. For example, if you wanted to change a person's phone number, Select the old phone number, and type the new phone number in. It automatically replaces the old one!

Creating a Page Break

Whenever you want to force a page break at a specific spot in your document, just press CTRL ENTER!

Cutting, Copying and Pasting Text

Windows based programs such as Microsoft Word all use the same basic procedure for moving around text. This can be done within the same document, a different document or even a different program (i.e. Excel). The procedure uses a temporary place in memory called **The Clipboard** to store the selection on and then pastes it wherever you want it. The selection stays on the clipboard until you put something else on it or exit Windows.

The procedure is described below. It is the same for cutting and copying with the exception of the second step. Cutting is like moving the text and copying will leave the original text there.

Cut & Copy

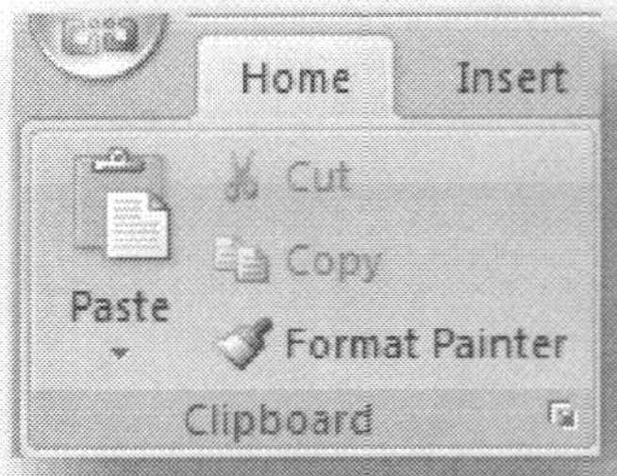

1. Select what you want to cut or copy.
2. Click the Copy/Cut tool or CTRL C or CTRL X or use your right mouse button to choose Copy or Cut.
3. Position the cursor where you want the text to go.
4. Click on the Paste tool or CTRL V or use your right mouse button to choose Paste.

   Watch for the "smart tag" after you've pasted in some of the programs. It gives you different ways to paste it (with or without formatting). This is very handy if you only want the text and not all the formatting that came with the original text (Choose Keep Text Only to do this)

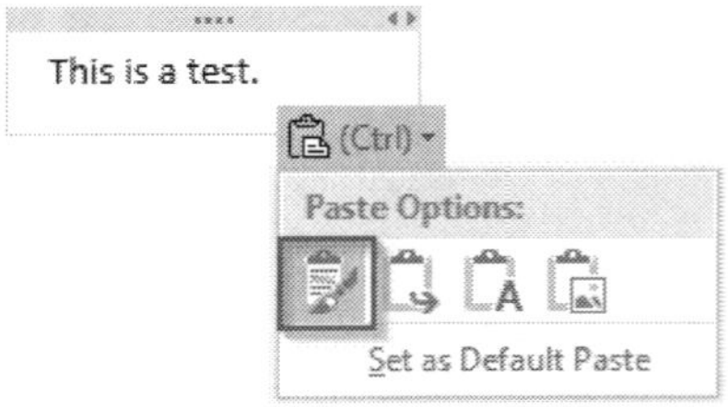

Drag & Drop

A short cut to cutting, copying and pasting is the **Drag & Drop** method.

1. Select the text you want to move or copy.

2. Place the mouse pointer anywhere on the selected text, then drag to move the insertion point where you want to move or copy the text.
3. To move the text to the insertion point location, release the mouse button.
4. To copy the text at the insertion point location, press CTRL and release the mouse button before releasing the CTRL button.

Printing

1. Click on the **File** menu button and click on **Print**.

The PRINT dialog box is described:

A preview of the document as it will be printed appears along the right side of this window.

Click this button to begin printing.	Print
Click this button to select the printer you want to use.	Brother HL-2170W Ready
Printer Properties Click this item to access additional properties for the printout.	
Use this section to specify which page(s) should be printed.	Print All Pages The whole thing
To specify certain pages to print, type in the page number or the range.	Pages:
Specify whether you want a single-sided or double-sided printout.	Print One Sided Only print on one side of th...
You can choose to collate multi-page documents so you don't have to go back and arrange them manually.	Collated 1,2,3 1,2,3 1,2,3
Choose whether you are printing landscape or portrait.	Portrait Orientation
Use this section to specify your paper size.	Letter 8.5" x 11"
Set your margins for the printout.	Normal Margins Left: 1" Right: 1"
If you're creating a booklet, you may need this to combine pages on a single sheet.	1 Page Per Sheet
Page Setup Provides detailed document settings.	
Use this section to zoom in and out of the document.	52% − +
Use this button to quickly display the full page.	
Use this section to move between pages within the print preview.	◀ 5 of 15 ▶

Enhancing Text

This module is designed to teach you how to enhance the appearance of your printed documents. The most common text enhancements (attributes) include: **Centre, Bold, Underline, and Font** changes. When used correctly, these enhancements will improve the legibility and aesthetic appearance of the printed page.

The Home Ribbon Tab

The Home Ribbon Tab allows you to choose commonly used formatting commands with the mouse either before or after you type the text.

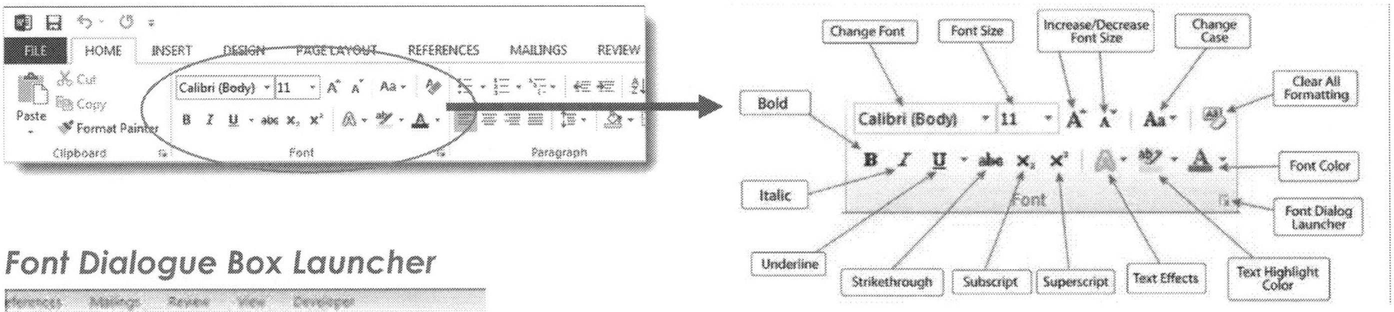

Font Dialogue Box Launcher

In order to access additional options, click on the arrow at the bottom right corners of the groups. There is one for the Paragraph Dialog box as well which is useful for setting line spacing.

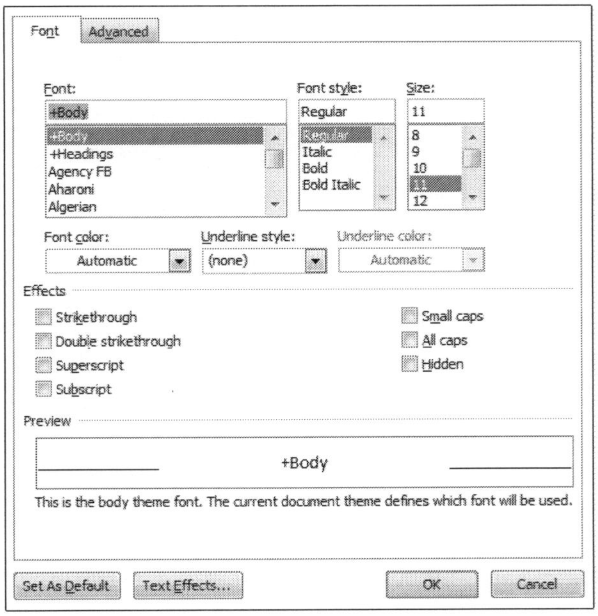

The Font Menu

When you wish to select more than one font change at a time or preview the font change first, you can use the Font menu.

Following are printed samples of the styles and effects listed.

Bold	**This is bolded**
Italic	*This is an italic font*
Italic Bold	***This is bolded and italicized***
Single Underline	This is singled underlined.
Underlined - Words Only	This is underlined - Words only
Double Underline	This is Double Underlined font
Dashed Underline	This is a dashed underlined
Color	Colored text will appear as black on a black and white printer. You must have a color printer to see colored text on paper. It will be colored on your screen though.
Strikethrough	~~This is a strikethrough font.~~
Double Strikethrough	~~This is double strikethrough.~~
Superscript	ie: McNally
Subscript	i.e. $H_{2}0$
Text Effects and Typography	There are a variety of text effects available.
Hidden	Text shows up on the screen but not when printed.
Small Caps	THIS IS A SMALL CAP FONT
	(it was actually typed: 'This is a Small Cap Font')
ALL Caps	ALL CAPITAL LETTERS.

Alignment

1. Select your text and click on one of the buttons below to align your text.

Left alignment is the default alignment. Text is lined up to the left margin. The right edge is called ragged because it doesn't line up to anything. The keyboard shortcut is CTRL L.

Centered text looks like this. It centers between the right and left margin and automatically adjusts according to how much text is typed. The keyboard shortcut is CTRL E.

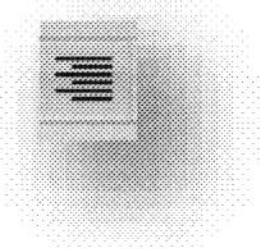

This text is right aligned as it all lines up to the right margin. The left edge is ragged, as it doesn't line up with anything. The keyboard shortcut to right align a paragraph is CTRL R.

Many people use Full Justification as it aligns text to both the right and left margins. This type of justification is used often in newspapers and letters. It makes a nice professional look. The keyboard shortcut is CTRL J.

If you just want to align one paragraph, you don't even need to select the paragraph. Just have your cursor in it somewhere and click on one of the above buttons!

Margins, Indents and Tabs

Microsoft Word allows you to change the margins and indents of your document in various ways. Both of these are done very easily using the Ruler.

Margins

Open SAFETY.DOC

There are many commands related to Page setup in the Page Layout ribbon tab. You can also get the following screen by using the dialogue box launcher.

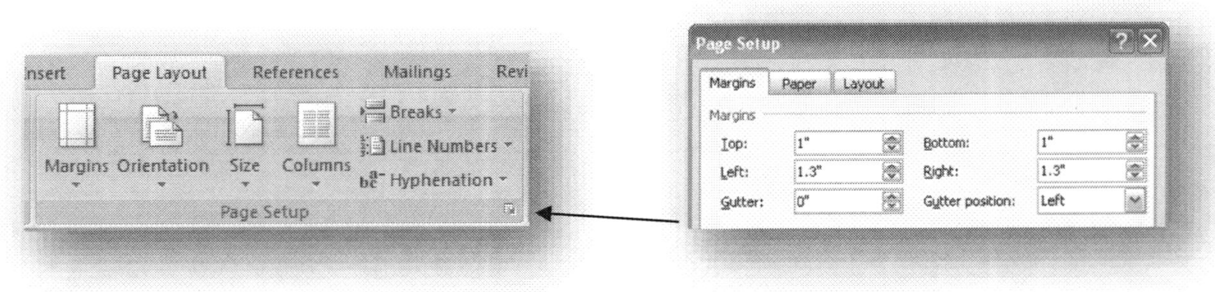

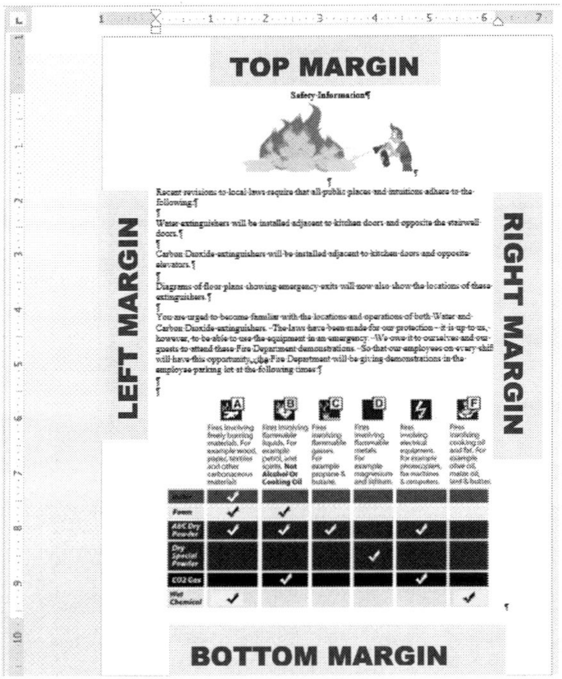

1. Bring up the Page Setup box and change the top margin to 2" and the bottom to 1.5". Notice that this change will affect the whole document.
2. Choose OK.

The Ruler

The ruler is designed as a quick and easy alternative to selecting many items found in the Format menu.

You can use it to set:

- margins
- indents
- tabs
- tables
- columns

If you can't see the ruler, click the Ruler checkbox on the View Tab on the Ribbon.

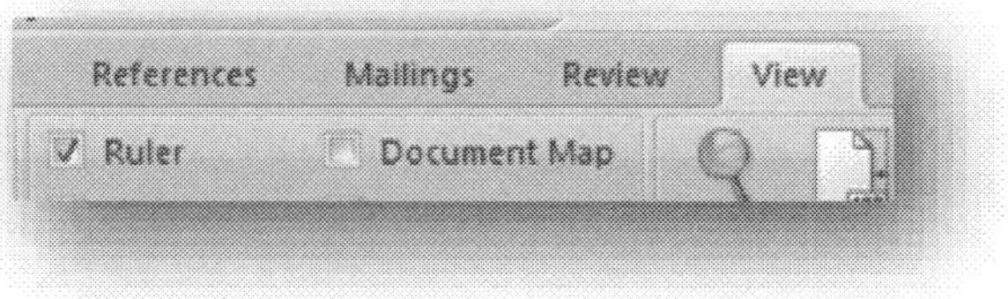

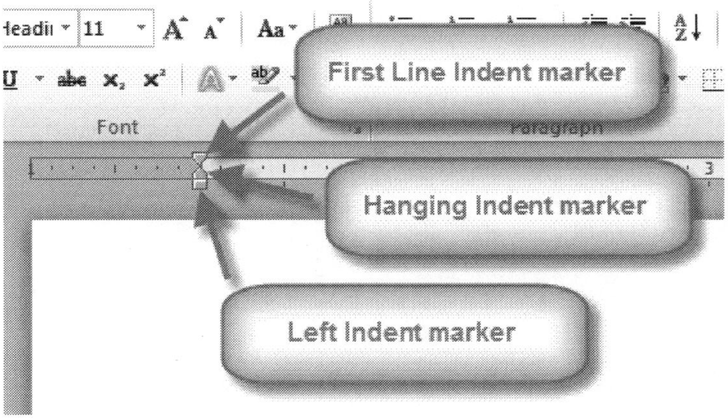

- **Left indent marker** - all lines in the paragraph line up with it. To move it Click and drag the box on the bottom of the marker.

- **First Line Indent** - The top part alone indicates where the first line of the paragraph is to start. To move it, just Click and drag it.

- **Hanging Indent** - the bottom part indicates where all other lines in the paragraph will start. To move it, click on the upper part of it, not the box, and drag it.

- Right Indent - this part is where the text wraps on the right side of the page. It moves by clicking and dragging it.

Indents

Indenting sets a temporary left margin at the next tab marker. When you use **Indent** the word wrap feature is in effect and you should not press the ENTER key at the end of each line.

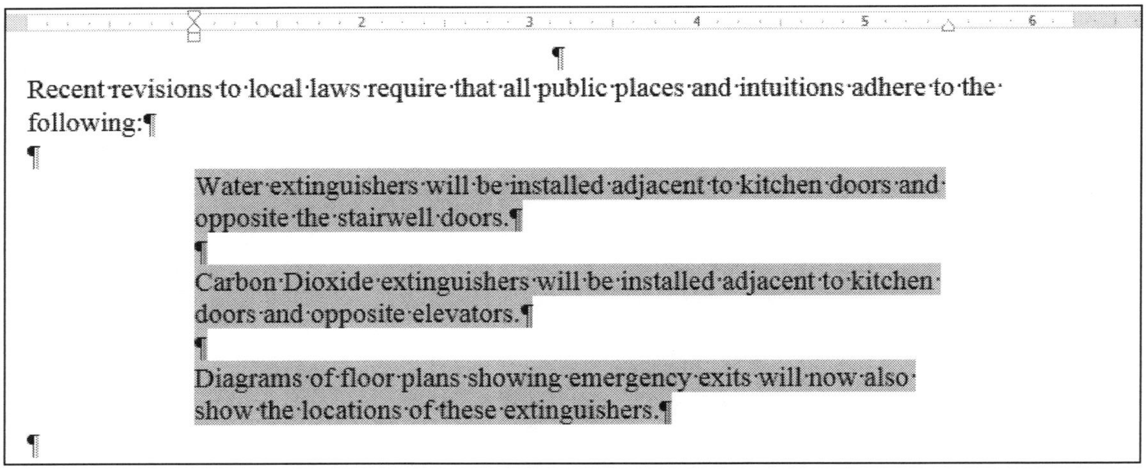

Decrease and Increase Indent buttons

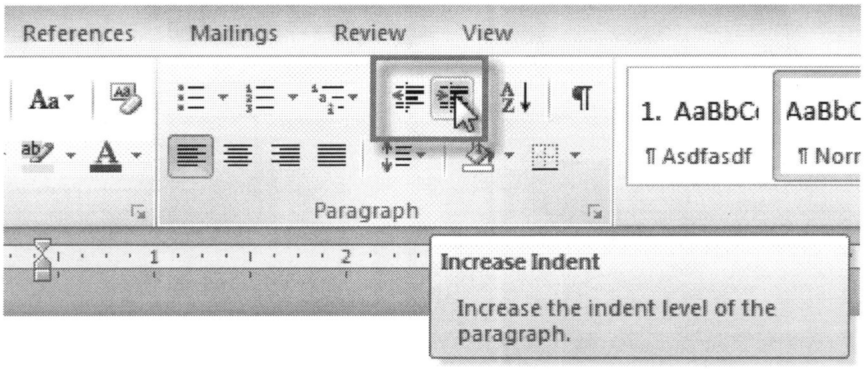

1. Select the three paragraphs starting at the word – Water.
2. Click on the Increase Indent tool on the Home ribbon tab or drag the left indent maker by the box at the bottom.
3. Click on the **Decrease Indent** tool next to it to send it back half an inch.

CTRL M – Increases left indent half an inch
CTRL SHIFT M – Decreases left indent half an inch

Hanging Indents

To create a different effect, we create hanging indents. We are going to add the following paragraph and apply a hanging indent.

[CTRL] [T]– Increases hanging indent half an inch
[CTRL] [SHIFT] [T] – Decrease hanging indent by half an inch

You can drag the hanging indent marker to move all the lines except the first line over. It will also move where you have hit the [TAB] key (after 8:00 AM).

8:00 a.m.	Car Fires - The Northeast corner of the parking lot will be cordoned off at this time. The Fire Department will actually demonstrate protective measures you can take when encountering car fires.

1. Type 8:00 AM and press the [TAB] key and type the remainder of the above paragraph.
2. Press [CTRL] [T] and see how part of the paragraph has moved over.
3. Press [CTRL] [T] again two more times.

9:00 a.m.	Grease Fires - The Southeast corner of the parking lot will be cordoned off at this time. The Fire Department will show you how to extinguish fires which may occur in your kitchen at home.

4. At the bottom of the document, press [ENTER] and type 9:00 AM.
5. Then press [TAB]
6. Type the following text:

> Grease Fires - The Southeast comer of the parking lot will be cordoned off at this time. The Fire Department will show you how to extinguish fires which may occur in your kitchen at home.

Note: To change anything about the ruler, the key is to select the text you want to affect then click and drag the appropriate marker.

The Ruler should look like this:

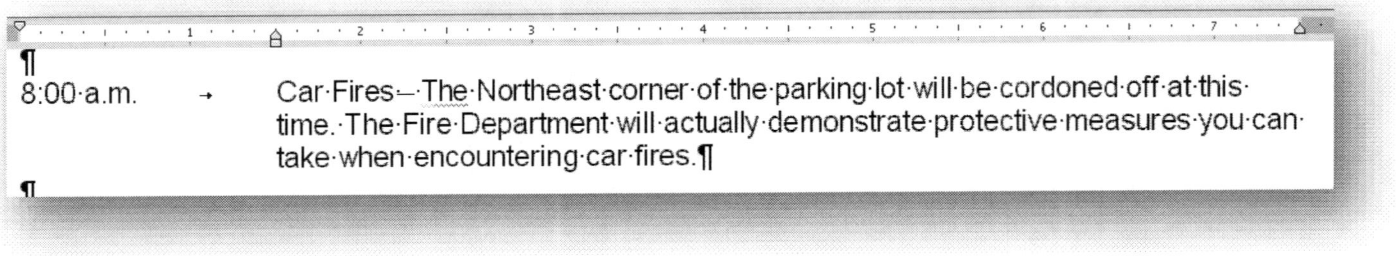

Removing Paragraph Formatting

You can easily reset the ruler and the formatting applied to a certain paragraph, for example if the hanging indent is no longer required. Simply select the paragraph and press CTRL Q.

This resets:

- Indents
- Hanging Indents
- Tab Settings
- Bullets
- Automatic Numbering
- Borders
- Shading
- Alignment (ie. Centering)
- Line Spacing
- Keep with Next
- Keep Lines Together

CTRL Q – Resets paragraph formatting

Tabs

Tab markers mark certain horizontal positions to align columns of text automatically. The printer recognizes these markers as exact positions and will line up text perfectly. If spaces are used in place of tabs, text <u>may not</u> line up correctly when proportionally spaced fonts are used.

There are four types of **tab markers** available in Microsoft Word. Each aligns text differently. Each type of marker can have **dot leaders.** Each type of tab is represented by a symbol.

	LEFT	CENTER	RIGHT	DECIMAL

Computer →	Computer →	Computer →	Computer →	$9.00¶
Monitor →	Monitor →	Monitor →	Monitor →	$99.00¶
Printer →	Printer →	Printer →	Printer →	$19.00¶
Mouse →	Mouse →	Mouse →	Mouse →	$399.00¶

It is simple to add tabs to your ruler.

1. Type the text or select the paragraph to add tab settings to. If the text already exists, you must have one tab in between each column.
2. Select the type of tab you want by clicking on the Tab Selector to the left of the left indent marker on the ruler until you see the desired one.
3. Click on the bottom part of the ruler wherever you want the tab to appear.

Before you set your tabs, clear your ruler by selecting your paragraphs and pressing CTRL Q to ensure there are no previous tab settings on the selected paragraphs.

To type the above list:

4. Type each line with one TAB in between each piece of text.
5. Select all four lines.
6. Ensure that the TAB Selector is set for a Left Aligned tab (L).
7. Click under 1.5 " on the ruler to place a 1.5" left tab.
8. Click on the TAB Selector until it is a center tab.
9. Click under the 3" on the ruler.
10. Click on the TAB Selector until it is a right tab.
11. Click under the 4.5" on the ruler.
12. Click on the TAB Selector until it is a Decimal tab.
13. Click under the 5.5" on the ruler.

Practice

Type the following line and set a right tab.

Memo	Effective Immediately

Your ruler should look like this (one right aligned Tab):

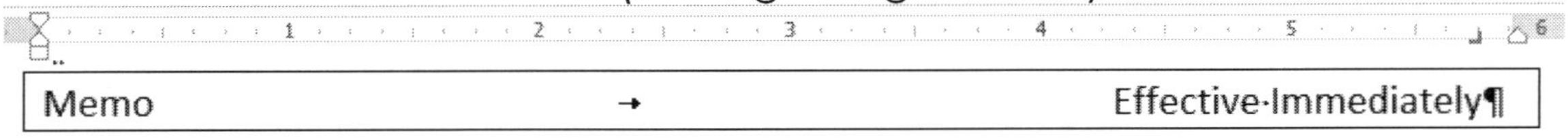

Open Tab Exercise1 and set the appropriate tabs.

Department	Employee Name	Local
Administration	Sandy Robert	7896
Word Processing	Donna Allen	6544
Switchboard	Tammy Richards	0

Your ruler should look like this (one left tab and one right or decimal Tab):

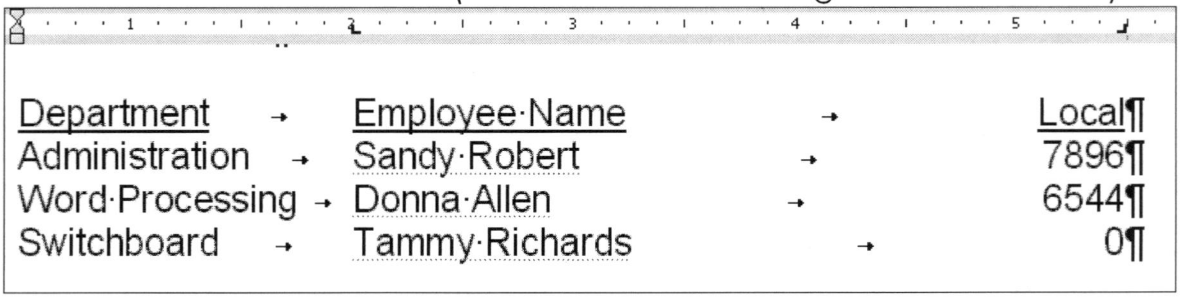

Line Spacing

Open TRAVEL.DOC

You can apply line spacing either before or after every paragraph or between every line within the paragraph. See how the following document can be spaced out using these options.:

TRAVEL SPECIAL:
Mexican Computer Cruise: One hour college credit while you vacation! Available to any and all CompAir employees who are eligible to participate. This six-day voyage masters the art of combining business with pleasure. Spend your mornings learning to use computers and your afternoons skin diving or sunbathing. Special attractions include shopping sprees in Mazatlan and Acapulco, with exquisite Mexican dining every night. Package includes cruise, air fare and one night's lodging on shore. CompAir employees are eligible to participate in special travel programs as set forth on page 37 of the CompAir Employee Handbook:
'Any employee who has been with the company for more than one year, and who has received at least one merit award, shall be eligible to participate in all special travel programs."

Before and After Spacing

TRAVEL SPECIAL

Mexican Computer Cruise: One hour college credit while you vacation! Available to any and all CompAir employees who are eligible to participate.

This six-day voyage masters the art of combining business with pleasure. Spend your mornings learning to use computers and your afternoons skin diving or sunbathing.

Special attractions include shopping sprees in Mazatlan and Acapulco, with exquisite Mexican dining every night.

Package includes cruise, air fare and one night's lodging on shore.

CompAir employees are eligible to participate in special travel programs as set forth on page 37 of the CompAir Employee Handbook:

Double Spaced

TRAVEL SPECIAL

Mexican Computer Cruise: One hour college credit while you vacation! Available to any and all CompAir employees who are eligible to participate.

This six-day voyage masters the art of combining business with pleasure. Spend your mornings learning to use computers and your afternoons skin diving or sunbathing.

Special attractions include shopping sprees in Mazatlan and Acapulco, with exquisite Mexican dining every night.

Package includes cruise, air fare and one night's lodging on shore. CompAir employees are eligible to participate in special travel programs as set forth on page 37 of the CompAir Employee Handbook:

"Any employee who has been with the company for more than one year, and who has received at least one merit award, shall be eligible to participate in all special travel programs."

1. Select the whole document by triple clicking in selection bar or press CTRL A.
2. Go into the **Paragraph** dialogue box, available from the Paragraph dialogue box launcher.

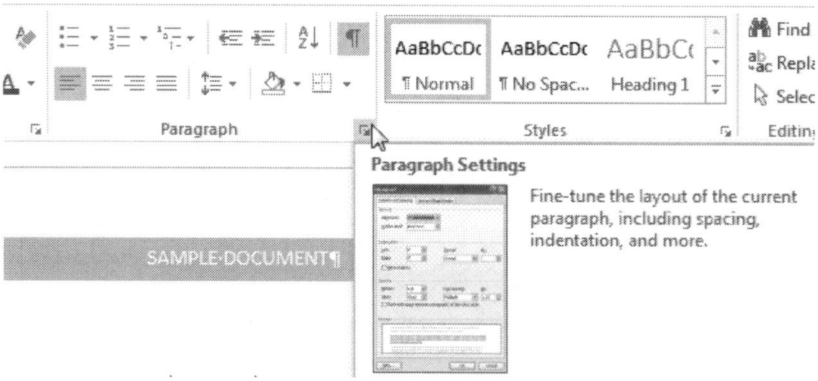

3. Click on the arrow beside Before to increase to spacing before each paragraph.
4. Repeat step 2 for line spacing After each paragraph.
5. Click on OK
6. To see how the Line spacing works, UNDO the last command to get the defaults back.

Uncheck this!

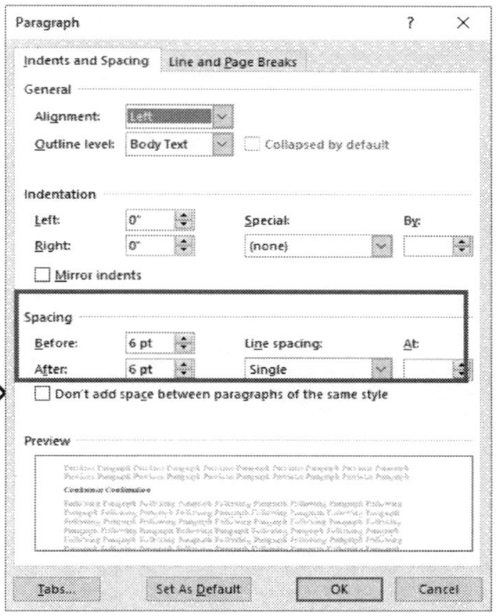

Now select the whole document and go back into **Paragraph** box and select Double from the Line Spacing list box.

If you would like all your new documents to have this setting, click on the Set as Default button!

Headers and Footers

There is an easy way to automatically have text such as page numbers, today's date or your company name appear at the top or bottom of every page of the document.

1. Go into the Insert ribbon tab.
2. By clicking the Header and Footer buttons, you can display a list of preformatted ones.
3. To create your own, choose Edit Header or Edit Footer.

   This brings up a toolbar that allows you to choose certain "codes" such as today's date and the page number. You can also type text in here.

   Use TAB to specify left, center or right alignment.

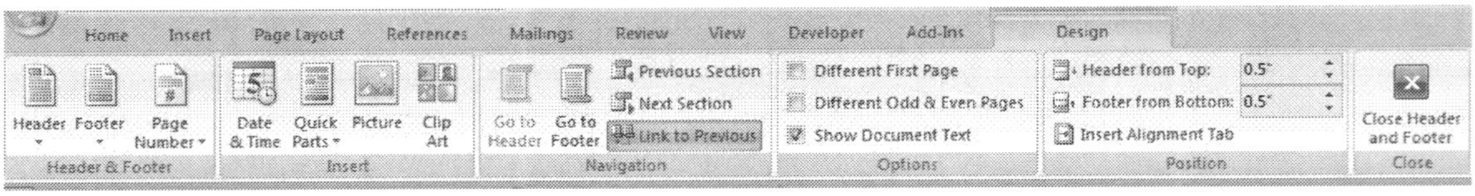

Notice there is an option if you want to have a different first page than the rest. This option is handy when you have a cover page and you don't want any headers or footers on it.

> You can quickly get into your header or footer by double clicking on the white space at the top or bottom of your page. If you already have text there, double click on that!
>
> Then to get out, double click on the body of your document!

Adding Page Numbers

1. To add a page number, position your cursor where you want the actual number to go.

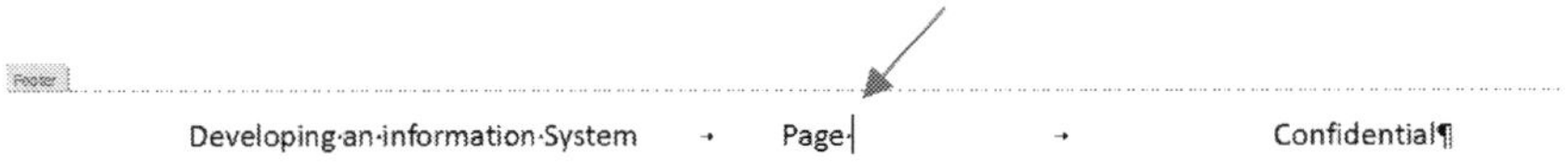

2. Be sure you're in the Header/Footer Design tab
3. Click on Page Number
4. Choose Current Position
5. Choose Plain Number.

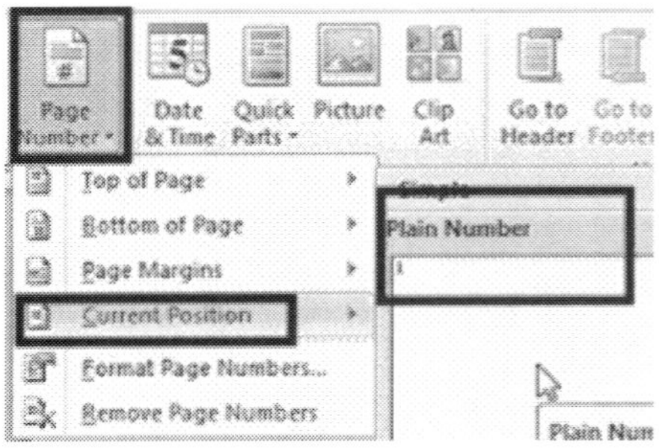

Bulleted and Numbered Lists

A quick and easy way to create a bulleted or numbered list is to use the built in Bullets and Numbering feature. This feature offers a quick way to "spruce" up linbe document.

Open LISTS.DOC

1. Select the four paragraphs starting with Bus ride to Banff .....
2. Click on the Numbering tool on the Home ribbon tab.
3. To make modifications to the number formats (i.e. Roman Numerals), click the drop down arrow next to the numbering tool to look at some predefined formats.
4. For more options, click on Define New Number Format. Here you can specify what to appear before or after the number as well as choose a number format.
5. To try out the Bullets feature, repeat the last four steps but click on the Bullets tool, beside the Numbering tool. Apply “Before and After Spacing” to add a great look!

- Bus ride to Banff from Edmonton. We will meet downtown at 5:30 Friday and arrive around 8:00.
- Welcome drink upon arrival at our welcome party on Friday night at our lodge. Get to know the people you will ski with all weekend
- 3 day lift ticket. You can ski on the best hills in Alberta all day Saturday, Sunday and Monday.
- Farewell drink on Monday at our Farewell party. Say good-bye to your new friends and make plans to meet again next year!

Changing a bullet from the default one:

1. Select all the paragraphs you want the bullet added to
2. Click on the drop down box beside the Bullets button.
3. Choose **Define New Bullet**.
4. Click on **Symbol** to see more bullets.
5. Once in this screen, you can change **Fonts** in the Font list box to see more choices of bullets. The **WINGDINGS** and **WEBDINGS** fonts give lots of interesting choices!

NOTE: When you are in a numbered or bulleted list and you would like a new line, but not a new bullet or number, use SHIFT ENTER instead to break up the line.

➢→A·bicycle·can't·stand·on·its·own·because·it's·two-tired.··¶

➢→Ability·is·what·you're·capable·of·doing...↵
Motivation·determines·what·you·do...↵
Attitude·determines·how·well·you·do·it.··¶

➢→A·bird·does·not·sing·because·it·has·an·answer·--·it·sings·because·it·has·a·song.··¶

Excel

Excel Screen

The Excel worksheet file, also referred to as a workbook, is an electronic spreadsheet that consists of a grid of columns and rows. There are 16,384 columns, labeled A through Z, AA through AZ, BA through BZ, and so on to XFD. There are 1,048,576 rows, starting at 1.

Each Excel file can also include over 255 worksheets. The worksheet name, which defaults to Sheet 1, Sheet 2, and so on, appears on a tab at the bottom left of the workbook.

The following diagram is of a standard Excel screen. Your version may look slightly different.

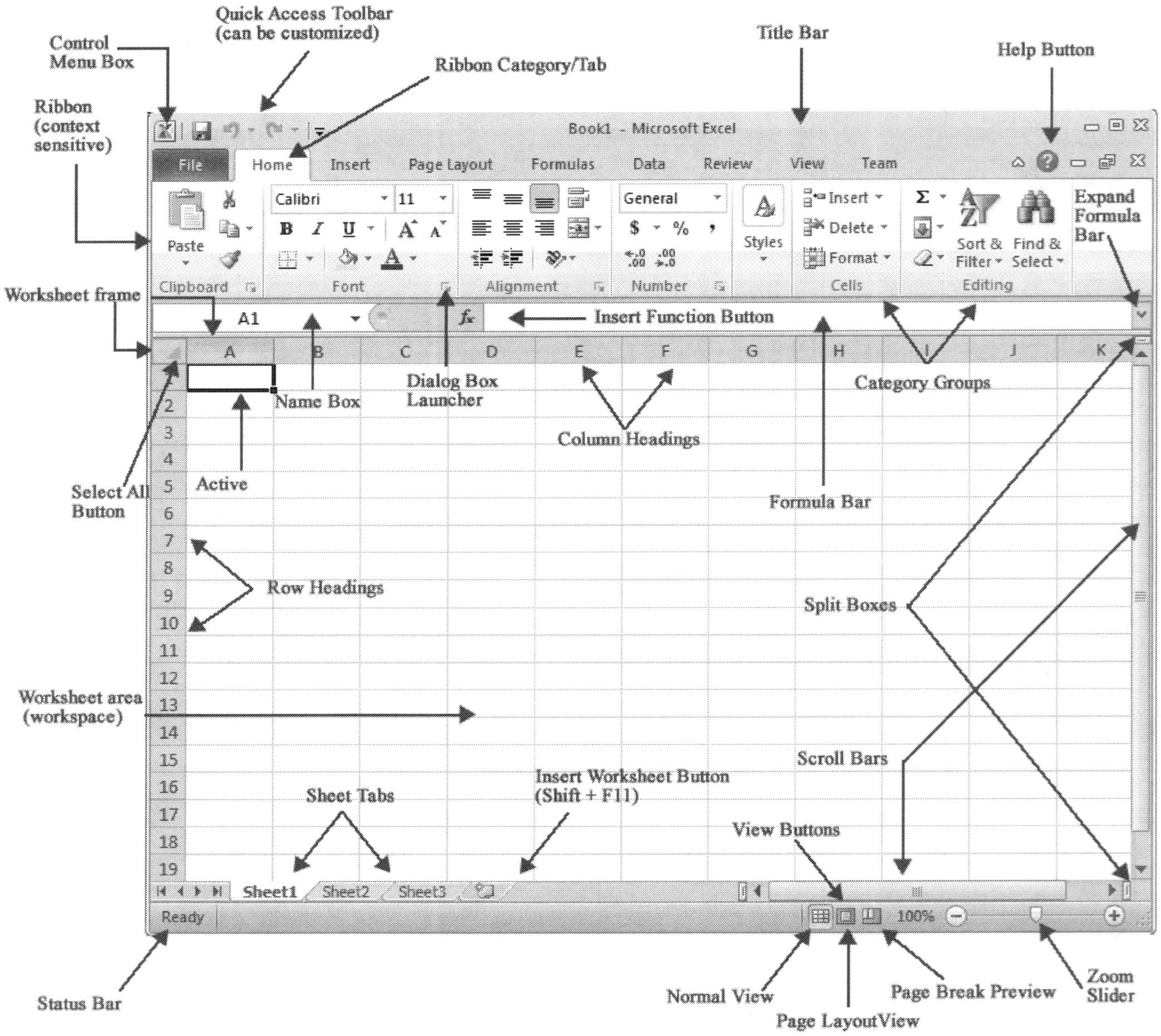

Some of the main components of the screen are discussed below.

Quick Access Tool Bar — Provide tools to access commonly used functions.

Ribbon — This holds many tabs that hold time saving buttons. For example, the Page Layout tab contains commands relating to setting up your print job. If you double click on one of the ribbon tabs, the ribbon will be minimized in order for you to maximize your work space. Double click it again to bring it back to normal size.

Active Cell — Highlighted by a rectangle. The address of the current cell appears in the **Name Box**. For example, A1 or C5.

Column Headings — Columns are given letters of the alphabet as names.

Row Indicator — Rows are given numbers as names.

Sheet Tab — Identifies the Current Worksheet.

Formula Bar — Contains the cell contents. This will either be a label, number or formula. Appearing to the left of it is the Insert Function button ***(fx)***, used for creating functions.

To add a button to your Quick Access Bar (the toolbar near the File menu), simply right click the button or menu item and choose Add to Quick Access Toolbar.

This bar stays on your screen whenever you're in the program, it never disappears!

Excel Cursors

1. Selection Cursor:

Click and drag to highlight multiple cells with this cursor, or click in a cell to select the single cell.

2. Autofill Handle:

Click and drag to fill in the other cells with content. It works differently depending on what you drag. For example, if you Autofill January, you will fill in the other cells with February, March, etc.

3. Move Cursor:

Click and drag the contents of the selected cell to any other cell.

4. Selection Bar (I-Beam):

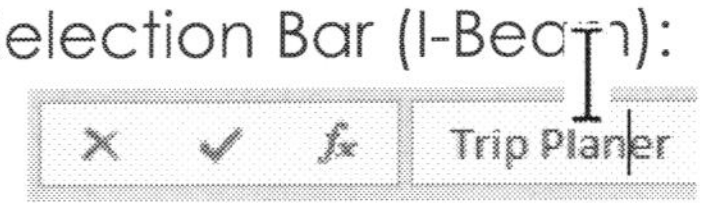

Click to place the cursor into the Formula bar so that you can edit an equation or function.

5. Column Width/Row Height Sizer:

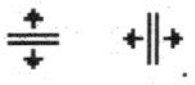

Click and drag in between columns or rows to resize them.

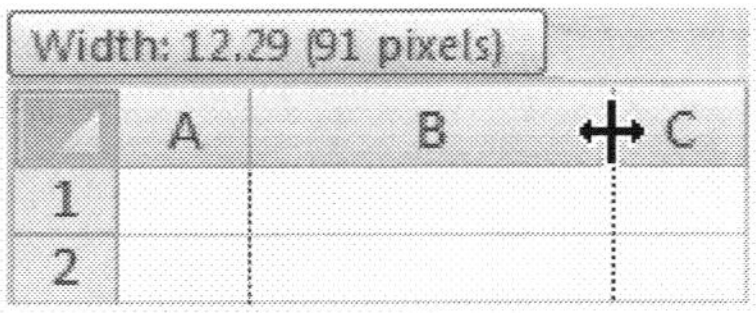

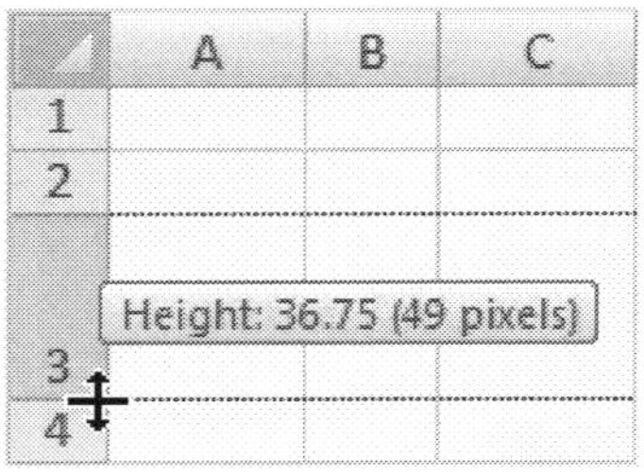

Double click when you see this arrow and it will automatically size your column or row to accommodate the largest entry!

6. Select Whole Column or Row:

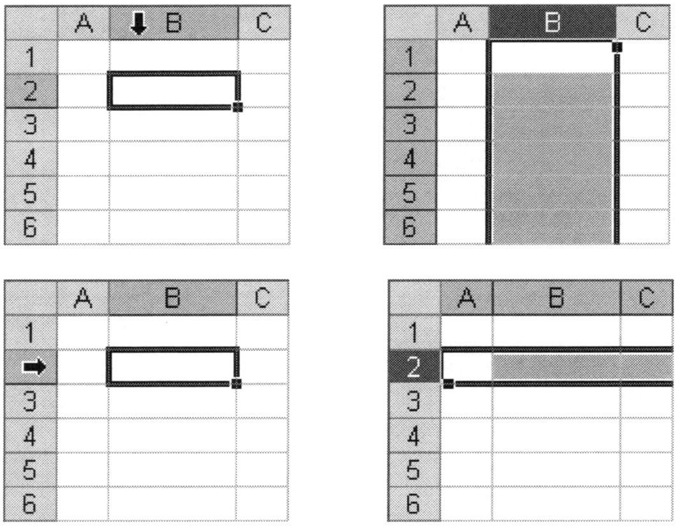

Click right on the Column heading or Row number to select the entire Column or Row.

Creating a Spreadsheet

Worksheets are created by entering data into cells. Excel recognizes three types of data: **Labels (text), Numbers, and Formulas.**

Labels

Labels are usually titles or comments. i.e. headings. As you type entries they first appear in the format line. Once you press ENTER or an **arrow key** they will appear in the **actual** cell.

- Labels can begin with any character except those characters which begin numbers & formulas.
- Labels can display across multiple columns if the columns are empty. If cells to the right of the label are blank, Excel displays the part of the label that overlaps those cells. If cells to the right of the label contain data, Excel truncates (cuts off) the label for cell display.
- If the first character of the data is ', A-Z, a-z, Excel assumes the entry is a label.

Numbers

Numbers are composed of digits and, if necessary, a leading minus sign and/or a decimal point.

- Numbers are automatically Right Justified.
- Numbers can also be aligned to the left, right or centre.
- Do not include any spaces or text in numbers.
- Numbers start with one of the following:

  1, 2, 3, 4, 5, 6, 7, 8, 9

- Numbers are considered to be values.

Formulas

Formulas are entries that calculate data. The result of a formula is a value.

The calculation can be a simple mathematical operation, such as subtracting one number from another, or a more complicated operation, such as determining a mortgage payment.

- Formulas are used rather than typing in actual numbers.
- Are arithmetic expressions referencing other cells.
- Formulas usually start with =
- Make sure you begin the formula where you want the answer to be.
- When entering the formula by the pointing method, you will need to press ENTER only once, at the very end of the formula.
- You can also type in only the cell reference after = (i.e. =B4) if you just want the contents of one cell to be in another. (i.e. carrying forward a total).

Arithmetic Operators

Simple Formulas
Always start with an = sign
+ Addition
- Subtraction
* Multiply
/ Divide

Order of Operation	
1.	(brackets)
2.	* /
3.	+ -

Examples:

=A1 + A2
=A4 * 7%
=D14-D15
=(B3 + B4) /2
=B10+B11-B12

Creating a Formula

Open
01D EXCEL BASICS

	A	B	C	D	E	F
1	Weekly Grocery List					
2						
3	Item	Quantity	Price	Subtotal	GST	Total
4	Bread	2	2.5			
5	Eggs	3	4.99			
6	Cookies	0	0			
7	Milk	2	5.13			
8						
9	Total					
10						
11	Weekly Bu	50				
12	Difference					

1. In cell D4, we will multiply the quantity by the price to calculate the total for that expense.

   On a calculator, you could input: 2 X 2.5

   In Excel, we enter an equal sign and substitute the numbers for cell names:
   =B4 * C4 and press 

   .

NOTE: You can also use the Point and Click Method to enter a formula.

To create =B4*C4:
- Click on cell D4
- Type the = sign on your keyboard
- Click on cell B4
- Type the * sign on the keyboard
- Click on C4 and press 

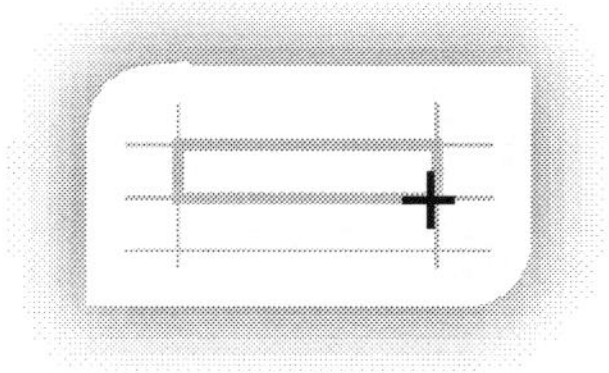

2. Since the next few cells (D5:D7), will have relatively the same formula, click on cell D4 and find the Autofill handle on the bottom right corner of the cell and click and drag down to cell D7.

   This copies and adjusts the formula down to the other cells!
3. Change the contents of cells B4. Notice the subtotal changes for that item.
4. Do the formulas for the GST and the Total and autofill them down.

   GST: =D4 * 5%
   TOTAL: =D4 + E4

Totaling Cells (SUM function)

It is very easy to total a column or row of numbers.

1. Click on the cell where you want the total to go. (D9)
2. Click on the AUTOSUM tool on the Home tab on your Ribbon.
3. Excel "guesses" at which cells you wanted totaled. If it is correct, just press ENTER. If not, click and drag over the cells you want included in the total. (D4:D8). You will normally want to include the blank cell so that if you ever insert a row between this range, the formula will automatically adjust to include the new entry.

	A	B	C	D	E	F
1	Weekly Grocery List					
2						
3	Item	Quantity	Price	Subtotal	GST	Total
4	Bread	2	2.5	5	0.25	5.25
5	Eggs	3	4.99	14.97	0.7485	15.7185
6	Cookies	0	0	0	0	0
7	Milk	2	5.13	10.26	0.513	10.773
8						
9	Total			=SUM(D4:D8)		

Format your numbers using the $ and , buttons

4. The formula should be as follows: SUM(D4:D8). The word SUM is an example of a function. This particular function adds the cells specified in the brackets. The part in brackets indicates this is a range of cells.
5. Autofill this formula over to add up the other columns (GST and Total).
6. You have budgeted $50 for the week. Do the formula to figure out how much is leftover.
7. How many cookies can you buy without going over your budget? They are $1.50 each.

	A	B	C	D	E	F
1	Weekly Grocery List					
2						
3	Item	Quantity	Price	Subtotal	GST	Total
4	Bread	2.00	$ 2.50	$ 5.00	$ 0.25	$ 5.25
5	Eggs	3.00	$ 4.99	$ 14.97	$ 0.75	$ 15.72
6	Cookies	-	$ -	$ -	$ -	$ -
7	Milk	2.00	$ 5.13	$ 10.26	$ 0.51	$ 10.77
8						
9	Total			$ 30.23	$ 1.51	$ 31.74
10						
11	Weekly Budget	$ 50.00				
12	Difference	$ 18.26				

To quickly see your formulas, try CTRL ~
(also referred to as CTRL TILDE or SQUIGGLE).

This command will show your formulas so you can troubleshoot your spreadsheet or keep an eye on your formulas to make sure they are working the way you want them to! Press it again to hide your formulas when you're done.
(The ~ key is on the top left corner of your keyboard, next to the 1 key.)

Practice:

1. On the Practice tab at the bottom, go to Sheet 2 and fill in the formulas wherever there is a shaded cell. Remember to autofill the formulas rather than recreating them.
2. Format the cells as either Accounting ($) or Comma (,). Adjust the numbers if necessary ←.0 .00 .00 →.0
3. Fix up the columns width and make it pretty!

The Completed Sheet:

	A	B	C	D	E	F
1	Trip Planner					
2						
3	Expense	Quantity	Price	Subtotal	Tax	Total
4	Flight	2	$ 350.00	$ 700.00	$ 35.00	$ 735.00
5	Hotel	7	$ 150.00	$ 1,050.00	$ 52.50	$ 1,102.50
6	Car Rental	1	$ 399.99	$ 399.99	$ 20.00	$ 419.99
7	Fuel	7	$ 20.00	$ 140.00	$ 7.00	$ 147.00
8	Meals	21	$ 10.00	$ 210.00	$ 10.50	$ 220.50
9	Entertainment			$ -	$ -	$ -
10	Misc			$ -	$ -	$ -
11						
12	Total Cost			$ 2,499.99	$ 125.00	$ 2,624.99
13						
14	My budget					$ 4,000.00
15						
16	Difference					$ 1,375.01
17						
18	Total Tax	$ 125.00				

The Formulas:

	A	B	C	D	E	F
1	Trip Planner					
2						
3	Expense	Quantity	Price	Subtotal	Tax	Total
4	Flight	2	350	=B4*C4	=D4*5%	=D4+E4
5	Hotel	7	150	=B5*C5	=D5*5%	=D5+E5
6	Car Rental	1	399.99	=B6*C6	=D6*5%	=D6+E6
7	Fuel	7	20	=B7*C7	=D7*5%	=D7+E7
8	Meals	21	10	=B8*C8	=D8*5%	=D8+E8
9	Entertainment			=B9*C9	=D9*5%	=D9+E9
10	Misc			=B10*C10	=D10*5%	=D10+E10
11						
12	Total Cost			=SUM(D4:D11)	=SUM(E4:E11)	=SUM(F4:F11)
13						
14	My budget					4000
15						
16	Difference					=F14-F12
17						
18	Total Tax	=SUM(E4:E11)				

4. Add some numbers for Entertainment and Meals but be sure to stay in your budget!

Autofill

To copy a formula or a value to the next cell or range of cells you can use the Autofill feature. This feature only works for cells that are adjacent to the cells you wish to copy. Excel will evaluate whatever you have selected and intelligently fill in the cells.

You can quickly fill cells with several types of data based on adjacent cells. When you click in a cell, notice that the lower-right corner is a black square. This is called the **fill handle**.

When you point to the fill handle the mouse pointer changes to a black cross. +

Click and drag the black cross to an adjacent cell to fill in the adjacent cell.

Text and numbers are copied to the adjacent cells. The cell references in formulas are adjusted to reflect the new cell location.

Examples:

If I type the following and Autofill across some cells:	I will get:
Jan	Feb, Mar, etc
January	February, March, etc
Mon	Tue, Wed, Thu, etc
Monday	Tuesday, Wednesday, Thursday, etc
Quarter 1	Quarter 2, Quarter 3, Quarter 4, Quarter 1, etc
Store 1 *	Store 2, Store 3, Store 4, etc
1st District*	2nd District, 3rd District, 4th District, etc
Elephant	Elephant, Elephant, Elephant
1000	1000, 1000, 1000
1/1/2008	1/2/2008, 1/3/2008, 1/4/2008, etc

*note: can be any word

This will overwrite whatever was in those cells so be careful when doing this!

Autofill Options

The Auto Fill Options button appears just below your filled selection after you fill text or data in a worksheet. When you click the button, a list appears to give you options for how to fill the text or data.
The available options depend on the content you are filling and the format of the text or data you are filling.

You will see a number of Autofill Options when you click on the box at the end of an Autofill action.

One of the AutoFill options may be to 'Fill Series.' By choosing this option, you will continue a series based on a pattern. For example, if you 'Fill Series' from a cell that contains the number 1, the next filled cell will be 2, the next 3, and so on for the number of cells filled. This forms a series in the filled cells where each subsequent number is the previous number plus 1.

1. Type 1 into a cell.
2. Autofill it to a few adjacent cells.

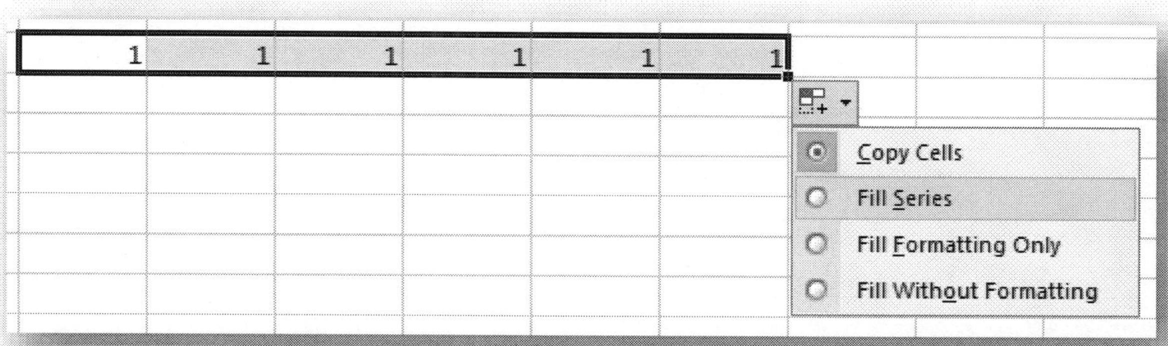

3. Use the Autofill options to specify it to Fill Series.

   It will increment each number by 1!

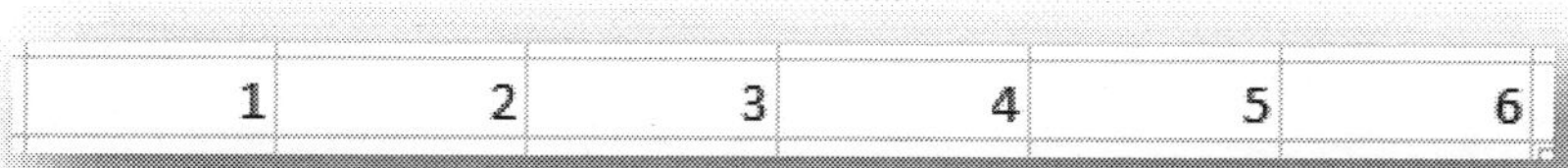

   In the next example, we will do the opposite -stop it from incrementing.

4. Type Jan into a cell and press ENTER .
5. Click on that cell. Place the mouse pointer on the black box on the lower right comer of the cell (Autofill)
6. When it changes to a black cross, click and drag it across or down a few cells. Watch the navigator as you are dragging.

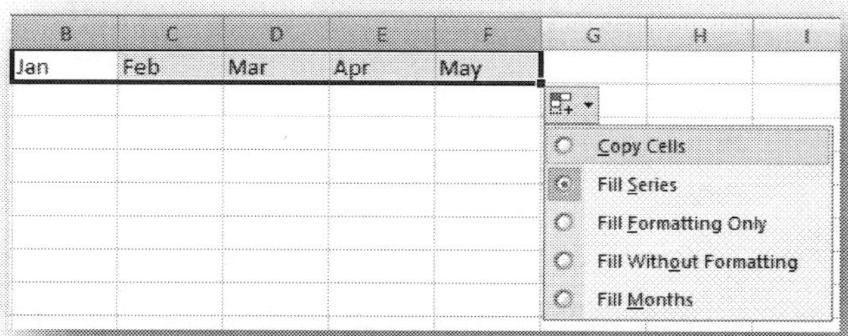

7. If you had wanted it to simply fill the cells with Jan, then you would use the Smart Tag Autofill Options to specify "Copy Cells" to override the default (Fill Series).

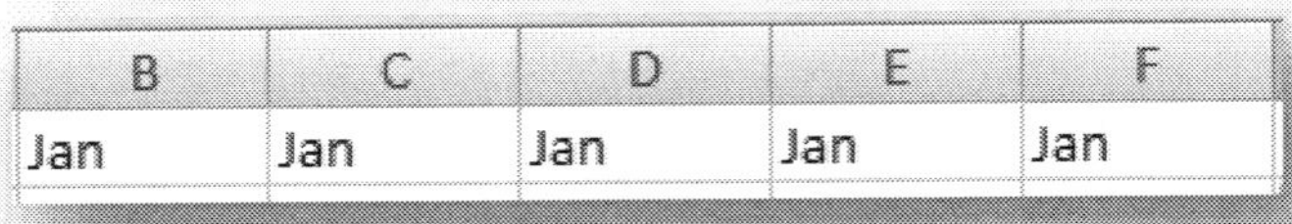

8. Try it with a date and you will see even more options!

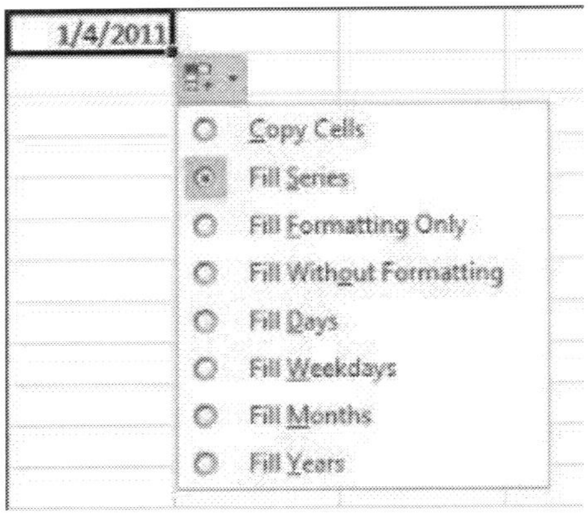

Autofilling a Pattern

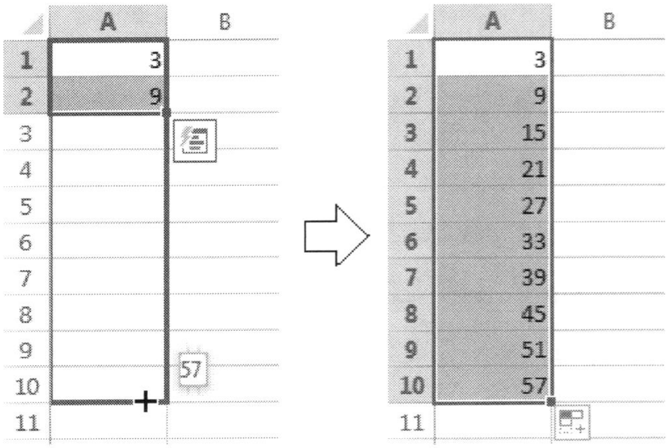

If Autofill doesn't give you the pattern you're looking for, you can create a pattern.

1. Type the first two entries in, for example if you want to increase each number by 6 starting at 3.
2. Then type 3 in one cell, then 9 in the next cell.
3. Next, select those two cells, let go of the mouse and autofill the selected cells to the cells you want the new numbers to go into.

Autofilling Formulas

When autofilling a formula, Excel automatically adjusts the formula.

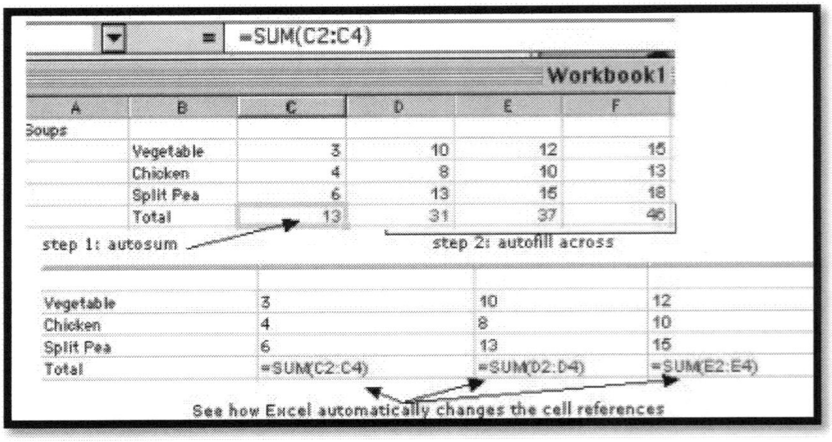

Editing Cells

Changing information in existing cells can be done in one of three ways:

1. If you are entering data in a cell, and have not yet pressed the ENTER key, then <Backspace> over the incorrect keystrokes.

2. Retype the cell information. This method is used to edit cells with very few characters i.e. numbers (12334). It will overwrite anything already entered into that cell.

3. Go into <Edit> mode.

- Double click on the cell and make the changes to the cell - OR
- Click on the cell you want to edit and then click on the formula bar - OR
- Press F2 and make the changes to the cell.

4. Type the new information and press ENTER. The previous contents of the cell will be replaced.

- This can be extremely useful for cells containing long labels or numbers, or complicated formulas.

- While in an edit mode, either the mouse or keyboard can be used for cursor movement.

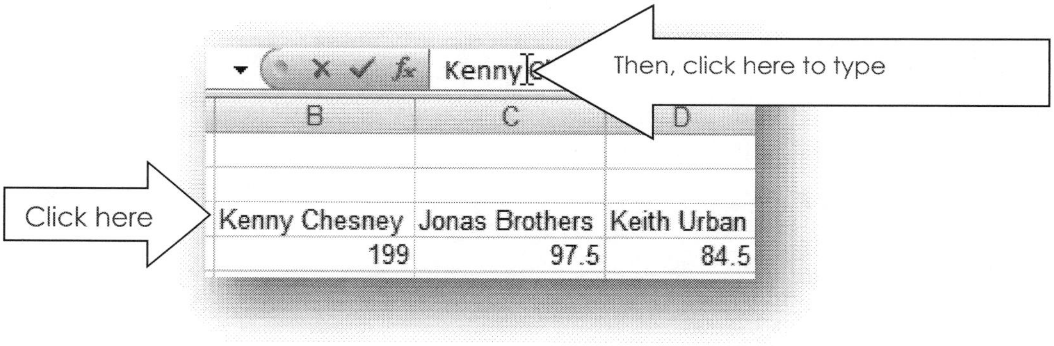

Formatting Cells

Numeric Cells

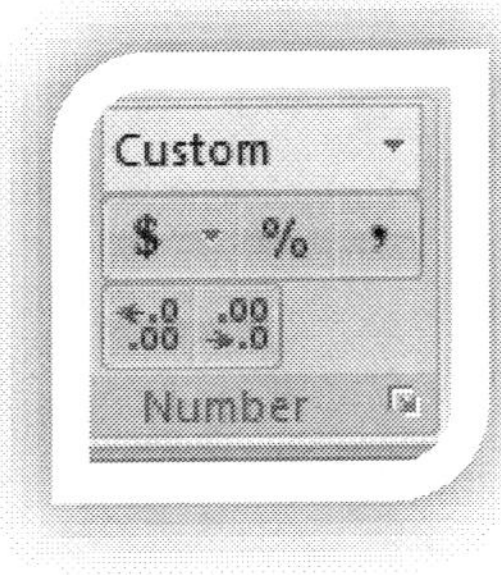

There are a few buttons on the ribbon that make formatting a breeze. You never need to worry about typing a dollar sign, a comma or zeros after your decimal place.

For example, you could just type 10 into a cell and have it appear as $10.00.

	Accounting Style - Formats selected text to display with a dollar sign and two decimals
	Percent Style - Formats selected cells to display percent with no decimal places
	Comma Style - Formats selected cells to display commas in large numbers as well as two decimal places
	Increase Decimal - Increases the number of decimals displayed after the decimal point
	Decrease Decimal - Decreases the number of decimals displayed after the decimal point

1. Select a cell with a number in it.
2. Click on the button with the Dollar sign on it.
   See how it adds two decimal places and a dollar sign.
   If it's 1,000 or higher, it will add a comma.
   If it contains a zero, it will show up as a dash.

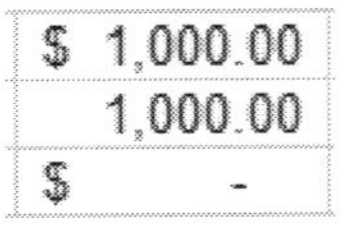

3. Click on the Comma button. It looks the same but loses the dollar sign.
4. If you do not desire that many decimal places, you can use the Increase Decimal or Decrease Decimal buttons to get the result that you want.

If you would like to get the number back to the way it was typed in, click on the Number Format drop down box and choose **General**. It may display Text, Custom, Accounting, etc.

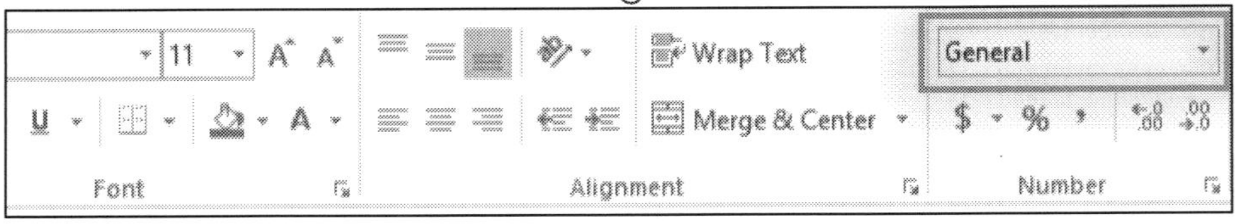

Formatting Date Cells

As long as you enter a valid date into a cell so that Excel recognizes it to be a date, you can have it display any way you like. You can tell how your computer is set up by typing in a date that is only valid one way, for example Christmas. Only one of the following is valid: 12/25 or 25/12.

If the computer is set up for month/day/year, then 12/25 will display as 25-Dec. Otherwise, it will show up as 25/12 and will not be recognizable as a date to Excel.

If you do this test and decide you don't like the way your computer is configured, you can go in to the Control Panel of Windows and choose Regional and Language settings (this might be worded differently depending on which version of Windows you have) and make the change there.

Once you're familiar with the format of how you can enter the date in, then you can change how it is displayed. For these examples, we will assume the computer is set to month/day/year.

For example, if I type in 12/25/03, I can have it display any of the following ways, just to list a few:

- December 25, 2003
- Dec 25, 2003
- 12/25/03
- 25/12/03
- 25-Dec-2003
- 25-Dec-03

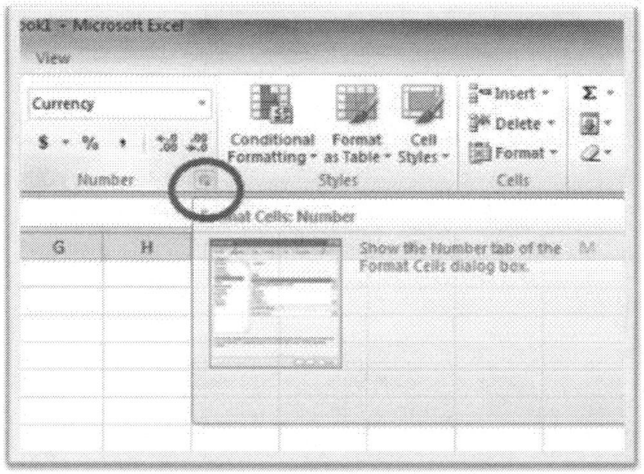

1. Select the cells containing the dates.

2. You can choose from the formats listed in the Number Format box on the toolbar or bring up the Format Cells dialogue box by clicking on the dialogue box launcher on the Home tab.

3. Click on the Date Category on the left. It will display some types for you to choose from on the right side. If you click on one, you will see a sample of it at the top of the box.

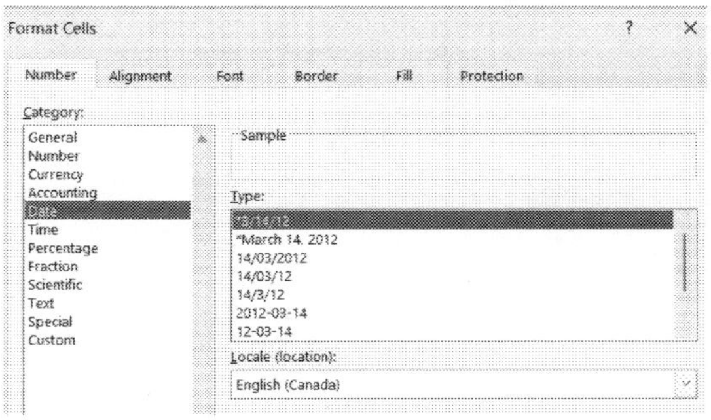

4. If it doesn't list the format you want, click on the Custom category on the left and you can type in your own format using placeholders.

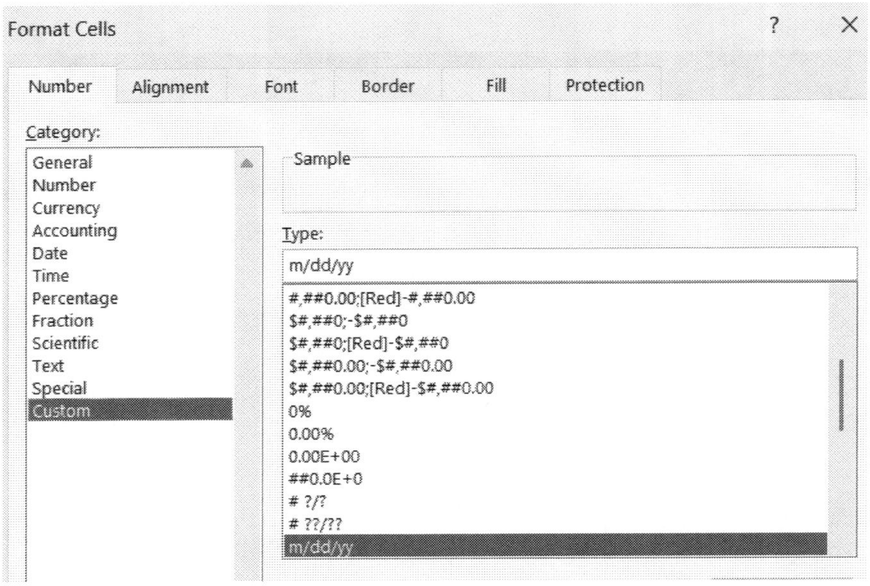

The following table lists some popular examples of different date formats.

Format	Result
m/d/yy	1/1/03 9/15/03
mm/dd/yy (extra zeros are added if necessary)	01/01/03 09/15/03 12/01/03 12/25/03
mm/d/yy	02/1/03 12/25/03
dd-mmm-yyyy	24-Dec-2003 01-Jul-2003
mmm d/yy	Dec 1/03 Dec 25/03
mmm dd, yyyy	Dec 01, 2003 Dec 25, 2003
ddd, mmm dd, yyyy	Sun, Apr 04, 2010 Thu, Dec 25, 2003
dddd, mmmm d, yyyy	Sunday, April 4, 2010 Thursday, December 25, 2003

Try right clicking on a range of cells to see some great options!
One is **Format Cells** which will also bring this dialogue box up!

Working with Columns and Rows

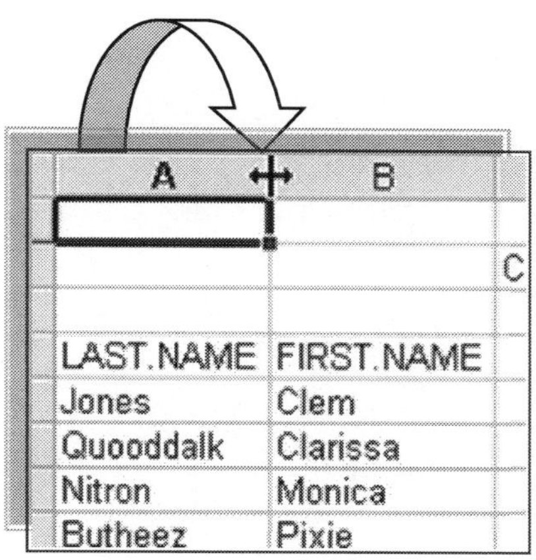

Column Widths and Row Heights

There are a few different ways to change your column width.

Autofit

Position your mouse pointer between two columns.

Double click when you see the double headed arrow. This makes the column on the left of your mouse pointer as big or small as it needs to be to accommodate all the information in it.

To change several columns, select the columns first, and then do the autofit on the last one of the selected columns.

Manually Size

With the same arrow, click and drag to manually size a column. To make several columns the same size, select the columns, then drag the last column and they will all be that same size.

Specify a Width

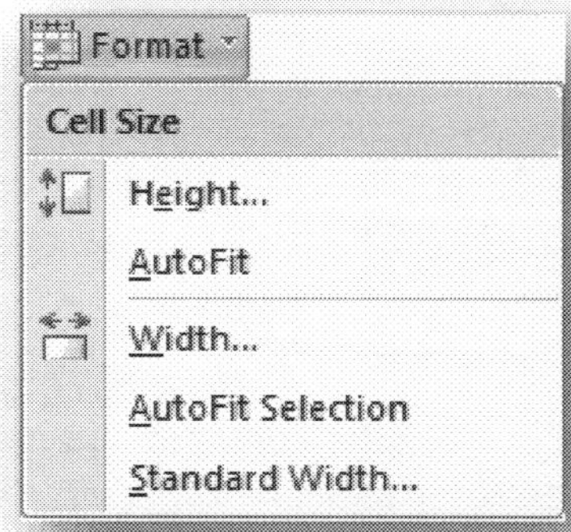

If you know the width that would like to make the column(s), select the column(s) and choose Format, Column Width from the Home tab. Type in a number for the selected columns.

Hiding a Column

Sometimes it is necessary to hide a column. With the same arrow as discussed above, click and drag it to the left until it is size 0.0. You can also right click and choose Hide.

Unhiding a Column

To unhide a column, take your mouse pointer to the line where the column should be and watch for it to become the same type of arrow you use to size and hide columns except that it will have a white line in the middle of it. Click and drag to the right when you see it and it will make the column visible again. 

Row Height

Basically all of the above information is the same procedure as with rows. If you move your mouse pointer to the line between two rows and click and drag, it will change the size of the above row.

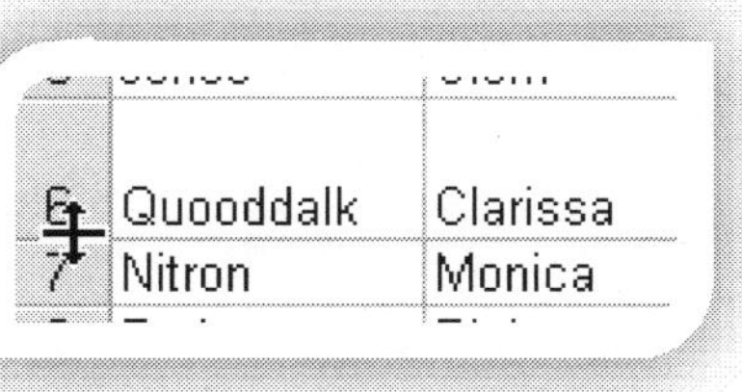

Inserting and Deleting

To insert a row or column, select the row or column you want to move down or over to the right. If you want to insert more than one, select the number of columns or rows you want to insert first.

If there is a blank row before a total row, select the blank row and choose Insert. This should adjust the SUM formula so that it includes the new row.

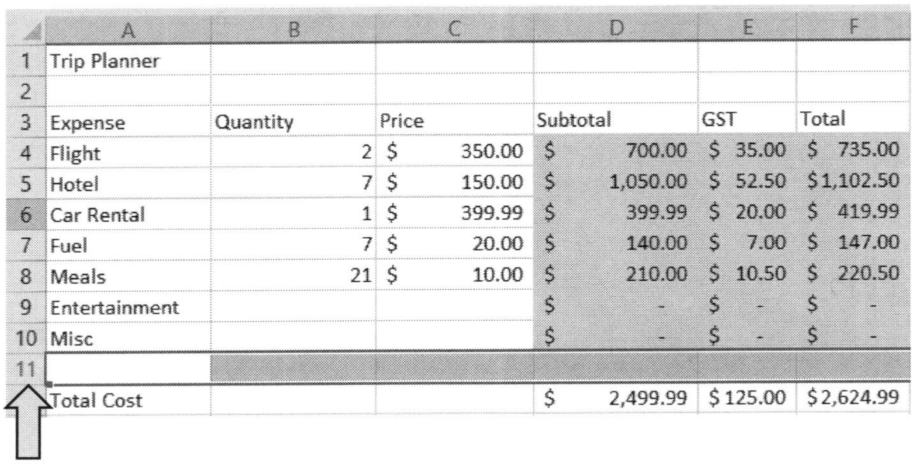

	A	B	C	D	E	F
1	Trip Planner					
2						
3	Expense	Quantity	Price	Subtotal	GST	Total
4	Flight	2	$ 350.00	$ 700.00	$ 35.00	$ 735.00
5	Hotel	7	$ 150.00	$ 1,050.00	$ 52.50	$1,102.50
6	Car Rental	1	$ 399.99	$ 399.99	$ 20.00	$ 419.99
7	Fuel	7	$ 20.00	$ 140.00	$ 7.00	$ 147.00
8	Meals	21	$ 10.00	$ 210.00	$ 10.50	$ 220.50
9	Entertainment			$ -	$ -	$ -
10	Misc			$ -	$ -	$ -
11						
	Total Cost			$ 2,499.99	$ 125.00	$2,624.99

1. Select a row or column.
2. On the Home ribbon tab, click on the Insert or Delete button. This will insert additional rows or columns or delete selected ones.

If you don't have a column or row selected, just a cell, it will delete just the cell you are on and may ask if you should shift the cells below it up or the cells to the right of it over.

Try right clicking on a range of cells and the Insert or Delete command comes up. Whichever option you choose will apply to whatever you have selected.

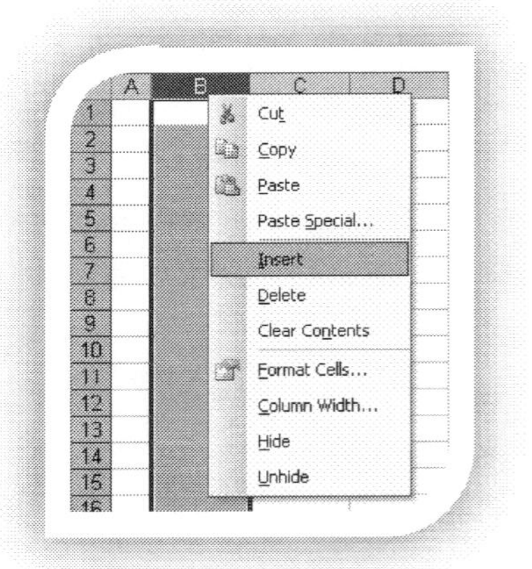

ie. Select a row, then Insert, it will give you a new row. If you had a column selected, it will insert a column.

If you just have one cell selected, it will insert a cell and push all the other cells down. Be careful with that!

Exercise

1. On the tab at the bottom of the 01D Excel Basics workbook, go to the sheet named Formatting Practice
2. Format the appropriate cells to look like the following:

	A	B	C	D	E	F
1			Apr 4, 2010			
2	PRINCIPAL	$ 24,000.00				
3	INTEREST	12.00%		$ 533.87	MONTHLY MORTGAGE	
4	LOAN TERM	60				
5						
6						
7		$ 23,000.00	$ 23,500.00	$ 24,000.00	$ 24,500.00	$ 25,000.00
8						
9	11.00%	$ 500.08	$ 510.95	$ 521.82	$ 532.69	$ 543.56
10	11.25%	$ 502.95	$ 513.88	$ 524.82	$ 535.75	$ 546.68
11	11.50%	$ 505.83	$ 516.83	$ 527.82	$ 538.82	$ 549.82
12	11.75%	$ 508.72	$ 519.78	$ 530.84	$ 541.90	$ 552.96
13	12.00%	$ 511.62	$ 522.74	$ 533.87	$ 544.99	$ 556.11
14	12.25%	$ 514.53	$ 525.72	$ 536.90	$ 548.09	$ 559.27
15	12.50%	$ 517.45	$ 528.70	$ 539.95	$ 551.20	$ 562.45
16	12.75%	$ 520.38	$ 531.69	$ 543.01	$ 554.32	$ 565.63
17	13.00%	$ 523.32	$ 534.70	$ 546.07	$ 557.45	$ 568.83

3. Type the date into cell C1 in the following format: m/d/yy. For example 4/20/10. Format it to a date format you like.

   For example, have it appear Apr 20, 2010.

   Try typing another date overtop.

Saving a Worksheet

Saving your work is one of the most important tasks you perform. Saving a worksheet file copies worksheet data from computer memory to a file on disk. If you do not save a worksheet file, the data is lost when you close the file or end Excel. It is a good idea to save the worksheet file often during the work session.

There are three ways to save new worksheets.

1. Save (on your toolbar or in the File menu)- opens the Save As dialog box and allows the user to type in a name. A default name appears in the text box but can be overwritten by typing in a new name.

   Excel automatically puts on the extension XLSX.
2. This can also be done by pressing CTRL S.
3. Choose **Save As** from the File menu button- does the same as Save on a brand new worksheet but creates a new file on a file that already has a name.

> Note…if you open an old spreadsheet saved in the previous version, it will automatically save back to that same version/format.
>
> If you create a new spreadsheet, it may be set to save in the new Excel format. This may cause problems if you are sharing spreadsheets with users who do not have this version (ie. clients, vendors, etc) as they may not be able to open them. You can use the Save As option to see the list of choices you have. Excel 2003 is readable by anyone with Excel but if you are using any new features of Excel they will be lost.
>
> 

You may be interested in saving your spreadsheet as a PDF. This will allow anybody with or without Excel to view it. Typically, they will not be able to make changes to it. Look in the Save as Type box in the Save As screen to choose this file format.

Formula Exercises

Open 01X BASICS PRACTICE.XLS

1. There are multiple exercises to do, each one in a different sheet at the bottom. You will see the instructions within the sheet. Each exercise has a corresponding answer sheet.
2. < > #1 #2 #3 #4 #5 #6 #7 #8 #9 #10 #1 Comp #2 Comp #3 Comp #4 Comp ...
3. After you have followed all of the instructions, click on the completed version of the exercises to compare your answers.

Additional Practice on Your Own:

1. Create a budget for yourself! It could look something like this. Be sure to put formulas in to do the calculations.

	A	B	C	D
1	**My Monthly Budget**			
2				
3	***Expense Type***	***Quantity***	***Cost***	***Total***
4	Mortgage	2.00	$ 500.00	$ 1,000.00
5	Utilities	1.00	$ 150.00	$ 150.00
6	Fuel	4.00	$ 50.00	$ 200.00
7	Groceries	2.00	$ 200.00	$ 400.00
8	Phone	1.00	$ 75.00	$ 75.00
9				
10	***Total Expenses***	$ 675.00		
11				
12	***Income***	$ 2,500.00		
13				
14	***Left Over***	$ 1,825.00		

2. Use Excel to track RSVPs the next time you plan event whether it be work related or personal. It could be a birthday celebration, dinner party, staff luncheon, a course you're organizing, etc.
3. Create a spreadsheet to track your user IDs and passwords. Make sure to password protect this spreadsheet!
4. Create a spreadsheet using one of the templates (File New) such as a calendar.
5. Create a spreadsheet for a trip you are planning on taking or have already taken. Include the cost of transportation, accommodation, meals and entertainment. Calculate what the total cost will be for the trip. Add an extra night to see how it affects the total. Upgrade your hotel room. Insert a row for travel insurance and see your Total Cost increase.

Relative vs Absolute References

Relative References

Open 02D-TIMESHEET ABSOLUTE

1. Enter the formulas for total hours and subtotal Pay and autofill them down. Notice how the cell references change.

   These are called Relative References.

	A	B	C	D	E	F	G	H	I	J
1									Vacation Pay %	0.04
2	Date								Annual Bonus %	0.1
3										
4	Emp#	Name	Mon	Tue	Wed	Thu	Fri	Total Hours	Pay Rate	Subtotal Pay
5	101	Jones	8	8	8	8	8	=SUM(C5:G5)	20	=H5*I5
6	102	Patterson	4	4	4	4	4	=SUM(C6:G6)	10	=H6*I6
7	103	Kozak	7.5	7.25	8	8	0	=SUM(C7:G7)	10	=H7*I7
8	104	Smith	7	8	8	4	8	=SUM(C8:G8)	10.68	=H8*I8
9										
10		Totals	=SUM(C	=SUM(D	=SUM(E	=SUM(F	=SUM(G	=SUM(H5:H9)	=SUM(I5:I9)	=SUM(J5:J9)

Absolute References

Sometimes we don't want the cell reference to change when it's copied. We need to make it "absolute" before it's copied so that it remains constant.

	A	B	C	D	E	F	G	H	I	J	K
1									Vacation Pa	0.04	Fuel Allowance
2	Date								Annual Bon	0.1	
3											
4	Emp#	Name	Mon	Tue	Wed	Thu	Fri	Total Hours	Pay Rate	Subtotal Pay	Vacation Pay
5	101	Jones	8	8	8	8	8	=SUM(C5:G5)	20	=H5*I5	=J5*J1
6	102	Patterson	4	4	4	4	4	=SUM(C6:G6)	10	=H6*I6	=J6*J1
7	103	Kozak	7.5	7.25	8	8	0	=SUM(C7:G7)	10	=H7*I7	=J7*J1
8	104	Smith	7	8	8	4	8	=SUM(C8:G8)	10.68	=H8*I8	=J8*J1

*=J5*J1 will keep J1 constant but will change J5 to J6 when copied down*

In this example, we are using cell J1 to hold the vacation pay rate. In the formula in cell K5, we will reference the cell name containing the rate, instead of the actual number (4%). This makes it easy to update if we think the rate will change at a later date – all we have to do is update one cell (J1), rather than all the formulas if we had typed the number into the formula.

To make a cell reference absolute, press the F4 key after you've entered the cell reference.

On some keyboards, specifically laptops, you may have to hold down the FN key while you press F4.

4. Enter the following into Cell K5:

   =J5*J1 and press the F4 key. Press ENTER.

5. Autofill it down.

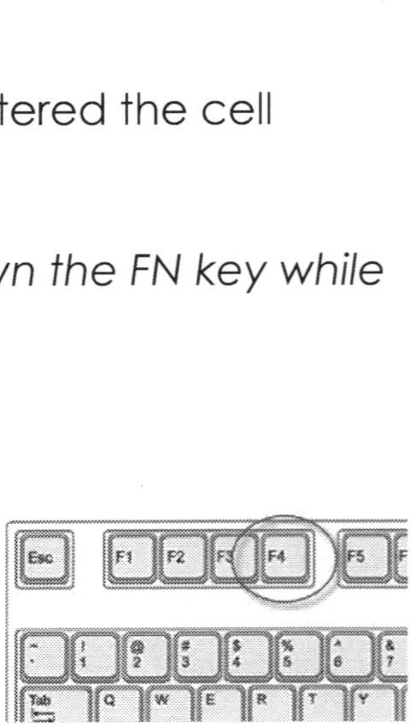

You will see dollar signs go around the J1 reference. Now when we copy that formula down to the next cell, the J5 will change to J6, but the J1 will not change because we have made it an absolute reference.

Common Functions

Open 03D ICE CREAM FUNCTIONS

Excel functions are built-in formulas that perform specialized calculations automatically.

Common functions are:

Function	Explanation	Syntax	Example
=SUM	Totals a range	=SUM(RANGE)	=SUM(B4:B27)
=AVERAGE	Averages a range	=AVERAGE(RANGE)	=AVERAGE(B4:B27)
=MIN	Lowest value in a range	=MIN(RANGE)	=MIN(B4:B27)
=MAX	Highest value in a range	=MAX(RANGE)	=MAX(B4:B27)
=COUNT	The number of values in a range (must be numbers present in the range in order to be counted)	=COUNT(RANGE)	=COUNT(B4:B27)
=COUNTA	The number of values in a range (if there is anything typed into the range, it will be counted)	=COUNTA(RANGE)	=COUNTA(A4:A27)

AVERAGE, MAXIMUM, MINIMUM, COUNT

The Autosum button has a drop down arrow that will allow you to choose the most common functions as listed above. If you want other functions not listed there, you will use the Paste Function tool.

1. Click where you want the function to go (B29). In this example, we'll create an Average.
2. Click on the drop down arrow beside the Autosum tool
3. Choose the function you want to determine.
4. Next, it allows you to specify the range of cells to evaluate. You can either click and drag over the cells or type them in. When you are finished, press the E key.

Do the same for MAX and MIN to get the highest and lowest values to appear.

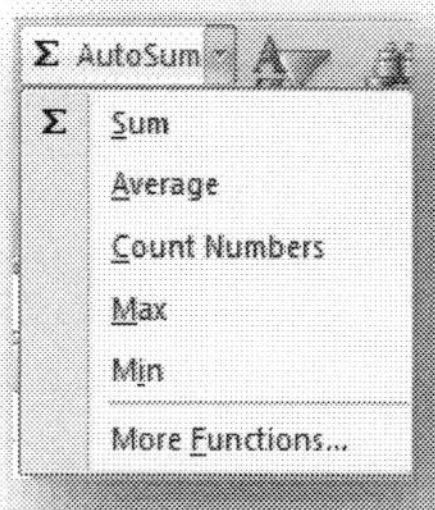

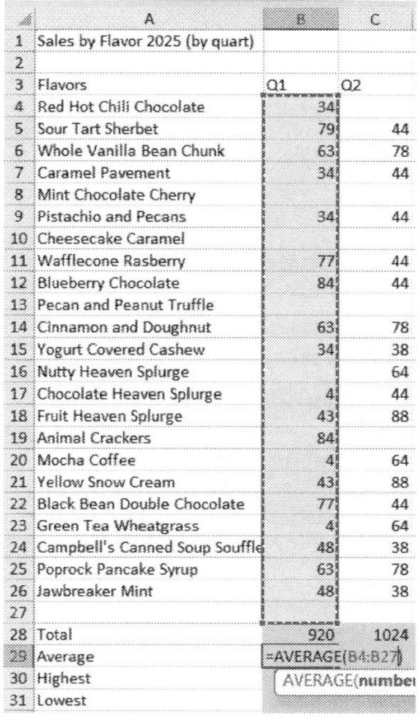

	A	B	C
1	Sales by Flavor 2025 (by quart)		
2			
3	Flavors	Q1	Q2
4	Red Hot Chili Chocolate	34	
5	Sour Tart Sherbet	79	44
6	Whole Vanilla Bean Chunk	63	78
7	Caramel Pavement	34	44
8	Mint Chocolate Cherry		
9	Pistachio and Pecans	34	44
10	Cheesecake Caramel		
11	Wafflecone Rasberry	77	44
12	Blueberry Chocolate	84	44
13	Pecan and Peanut Truffle		
14	Cinnamon and Doughnut	63	78
15	Yogurt Covered Cashew	34	38
16	Nutty Heaven Splurge		64
17	Chocolate Heaven Splurge	4	44
18	Fruit Heaven Splurge	43	88
19	Animal Crackers	84	
20	Mocha Coffee	4	64
21	Yellow Snow Cream	43	88
22	Black Bean Double Chocolate	77	44
23	Green Tea Wheatgrass	4	64
24	Campbell's Canned Soup Souffle	48	38
25	Poprock Pancake Syrup	63	78
26	Jawbreaker Mint	48	38
27			
28	Total	920	1024
29	Average	=AVERAGE(B4:B27)	
30	Highest	AVERAGE(number	
31	Lowest		

If you are doing a COUNT on non-numbers, ie. Names, you will have to add the "A" to the count to change it from COUNT to COUNTA.
Follow the same steps as COUNT, just add the "A" right before you press ENTER.

	A	B	C
2			
3	Flavors	Q1	Q2
4	Animal Crackers	34.00	
5	Black Bean Double Chocolate	79.00	44.00
6	Blueberry Chocolate	63.00	78.00
7	Campbell's Canned Soup Souffle	34.00	44.00
8	Caramel Pavement		
9	Cheesecake Caramel	34.00	44.00
10	Chocolate Heaven Splurge		
11	Cinnamon and Doghnut	77.00	44.00
12	Fruit Heaven Splurge	84.00	44.00
13	Green Tea Wheatgrass		
14	Jawbreaker Mint	63.00	78.00
15	Mint Chocolate Cherry	34.00	38.00
16	Mocha Coffee		64.00
17	Nutty Heaven Splurge	4.00	44.00
18	Pecan and Peanut Truffle	43.00	88.00
19	Pistachio and Pecans	84.00	
20	Poprock Pancake Syrup	4.00	64.00
21	Red Hot Chili Chocolate	43.00	88.00
22	Sour Tart Sherbet	77.00	44.00
23	Wafflecone Rasberry	4.00	64.00
24	Whole Vanilla Bean Chunk	48.00	38.00
25	Yellow Snow Cream	63.00	78.00
26	Yogurt Covered Cashew	48.00	38.00
27			
28	Total	920.00	1,024.00
29	Average	48.42	56.89
30	Highest	84.00	88.00
31	Lowest	4.00	38.00
32	# of Flavors Sold	19.00	18.00
33	# of Flavors Available	=COUNTA(A4:A27)	

NOTE: When you are specifying a range to include, make sure you include any blank cells that may be filled in at some point. The blank cell is where you would go to insert a new row, should you wish to add data. If the blank cell is included in your formula, your formula adjusts automatically to include the new row!

Completed:

	A	B	C	D	E	F
2						
3	Flavors	Q1	Q2	Q3	Q4	Total
4	Animal Crackers	34.00		88.00	94.00	216.00
5	Black Bean Double Chocolate	79.00	44.00	7.00	44.00	174.00
6	Blueberry Chocolate	63.00	78.00	89.00	34.00	264.00
7	Campbell's Canned Soup Souffle	34.00	44.00	88.00	94.00	260.00
8	Caramel Pavement			87.00	43.00	130.00
9	Cheesecake Caramel	34.00	44.00	88.00	94.00	260.00
.0	Chocolate Heaven Splurge			34.00	48.00	82.00
.1	Cinnamon and Doghnut	77.00	44.00	34.00		155.00
.2	Fruit Heaven Splurge	84.00	44.00	8.00	7.00	143.00
.3	Green Tea Wheatgrass				7.00	7.00
.4	Jawbreaker Mint	63.00	78.00	89.00		230.00
.5	Mint Chocolate Cherry	34.00	38.00	34.00	48.00	154.00
.6	Mocha Coffee		64.00	476.00	48.00	588.00
.7	Nutty Heaven Splurge	4.00	44.00	87.00	43.00	178.00
.8	Pecan and Peanut Truffle	43.00	88.00			131.00
.9	Pistachio and Pecans	84.00		8.00		92.00
:0	Poprock Pancake Syrup	4.00	64.00	88.00	48.00	204.00
:1	Red Hot Chili Chocolate	43.00	88.00	84.00	447.00	662.00
:2	Sour Tart Sherbet	77.00	44.00	34.00		155.00
:3	Wafflecone Rasberry	4.00	64.00	73.00	48.00	189.00
:4	Whole Vanilla Bean Chunk	48.00	38.00	6.00	48.00	140.00
:5	Yellow Snow Cream	63.00	78.00	89.00	34.00	264.00
:6	Yogurt Covered Cashew	48.00	38.00	6.00	48.00	140.00
:7						
:8	Total	920.00	1,024.00	1,597.00	1,277.00	4,818.00
:9	Average	48.42	56.89	76.05	70.94	209.48
i0	Highest	84.00	88.00	476.00	447.00	662.00
i1	Lowest	4.00	38.00	6.00	7.00	7.00
i2	# of Flavors Sold	19.00	18.00	21.00	18.00	23.00
i3	# of Flavors Available	23.00				

	A	B	C	D	E	F
1	**Sales by Fl**					
2						
3	Flavors	Q1	Q2	Q3	Q4	Total
4	Animal Crackers	34		88	94	=SUM(B4:E4)
5	Black Bean Doubl	79	44	7	44	=SUM(B5:E5)
6	Blueberry Chocol	63	78	89	34	=SUM(B6:E6)
7	Campbell's Canne	34	44	88	94	=SUM(B7:E7)
8	Caramel Paveme			87	43	=SUM(B8:E8)
9	Cheesecake Cara	34	44	88	94	=SUM(B9:E9)
10	Chocolate Heave			34	48	=SUM(B10:E10)
11	Cinnamon and Dc	77	44	34		=SUM(B11:E11)
12	Fruit Heaven Splt	84	44	8	7	=SUM(B12:E12)
13	Green Tea Wheat				7	=SUM(B13:E13)
14	Jawbreaker Mint	63	78	89		=SUM(B14:E14)
15	Mint Chocolate C	34	38	34	48	=SUM(B15:E15)
16	Mocha Coffee		64	476	48	=SUM(B16:E16)
17	Nutty Heaven Spl	4	44	87	43	=SUM(B17:E17)
18	Pecan and Peanu	43	88			=SUM(B18:E18)
19	Pistachio and Pec	84		8		=SUM(B19:E19)
20	Poprock Pancake	4	64	88	48	=SUM(B20:E20)
21	Red Hot Chili Cho	43	88	84	447	=SUM(B21:E21)
22	Sour Tart Sherbet	77	44	34		=SUM(B22:E22)
23	Wafflecone Rasb	4	64	73	48	=SUM(B23:E23)
24	Whole Vanilla Be	48	38	6	48	=SUM(B24:E24)
25	Yellow Snow Cre	63	78	89	34	=SUM(B25:E25)
26	Yogurt Covered C	48	38	6	48	=SUM(B26:E26)
27						
28	Total	=SUM(B4:B27)	=SUM(C4:C27)	=SUM(D4:D27)	=SUM(E4:E27)	=SUM(F4:F27)
29	Average	=AVERAGE(B4:B27)	=AVERAGE(C4:C2	=AVERAGE(D4:D2	=AVERAGE(E4:E2	=AVERAGE(F4:F2
30	Highest	=MAX(B4:B27)	=MAX(C4:C27)	=MAX(D4:D27)	=MAX(E4:E27)	=MAX(F4:F27)
31	Lowest	=MIN(B4:B27)	=MIN(C4:C27)	=MIN(D4:D27)	=MIN(E4:E27)	=MIN(F4:F27)
32	# of Flavors Sold	=COUNT(B4:B27)	=COUNT(C4:C27)	=COUNT(D4:D27)	=COUNT(E4:E27)	=COUNT(F4:F27)
33	# of Flavors Avail.	=COUNTA(A4:A27)				

Exercises

Absolute References:

Open 02X Absolute Practice

Functions:

Open 03X Functions Practice

1. There are several exercises to do, each one in a different sheet at the bottom. You will see the instructions within the sheet.

   The cells that required formulas are colored yellow.

2. After you have followed all of the instructions, click on the Completed version of the exercises to compare your answers.

Use CTRL ~ to check out your formulas!

Sorting your Spreadsheet

You can display database records in any order by sorting or rearranging the data. You sort information in a database according to the contents of a column or group of columns, called a sort key.

	A	B	C	D
1	House Prices			
2				
3	City	Purchase Price	Sold Price	Profit
4	Calgary	180524	450000	269476
5	Edmonton	127718	325000	197282
6	Regina	94205		-94205
7	Saskatoon	106248	104000	-2248
8	Toronto	255910	850000	594090
9	Vancouver	301228	752000	450772
10	Ottawa	158007	375000	216993
11	Montreal			0
12	Quebec City	97062		-97062
13	St. John's	100722	675000	574278
14	Halifax	118229		-118229
15				
16	Total			
17	Average			
18	Highest			
19	Lowest			

It's important that the spreadsheet is set up properly in order to sort your data properly.

1. No blank row between the heading row and the first row of data
2. There should only be one row of headings
3. No blank rows or columns within your data
4. There should be at least one blank row between your last row of data and your total row

Simple Sorting

It is very simple to sort by one column.

1. Simply click on one of the cells in the column you wish to sort by (ie. City Name)
2. Click on one of the sorting buttons, depending on if you want to sort by ascending or descending order.

Press CTRL A to test that your data is set up correctly. This will select the area that it will assume you want to sort.

NOTE: It is very important **not** to select any data and then hit the sort buttons, because it will only sort what you have selected and leave everything else as is!!

If you want to do any more complex sorting, simply click in your data somewhere and choose Custom Sort from the Sort & Filter button.

Printing

Open
04D NAMES PRINTING.XLSX

This module will teach you how to print from a worksheet file and how to preview your worksheet file before you print it. You will also change the Page Setup including options such as Headers & Footers, Margins, Orientation and Scaling.

Previewing Your Print Job

1. Choose Print from the File menu.

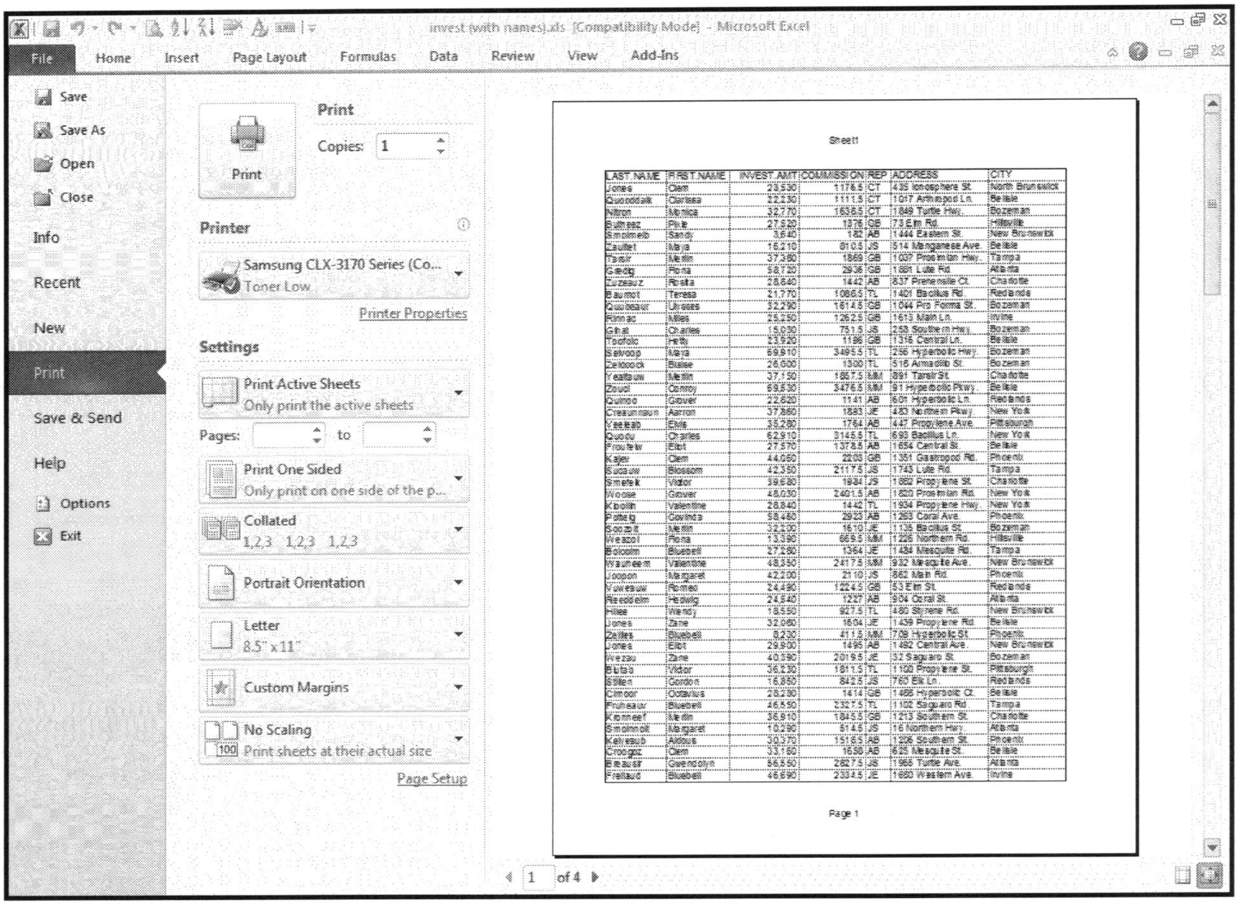

Many of the above features are on this screen, as well as a quick link to Page Setup. You are also able to perform other tasks right from this screen such as switch from portrait to landscape and choose a paper size. In the bottom right corner, you'll see a couple of buttons for showing your margins and Zooming in and out. To get out of this screen without printing, simply click on the HOME tab at the top on the ribbon or press the ESC key.

Page Setup

The **Setup** command lets you adjust page margins, include a header or footer for each page, and specify other print and layout settings.

1. Click on the Page Layout Tab on the ribbon or click on the Setup button if you're in Print Preview.

   There are four tabs in the Page Setup box. Following is a list of the options which can be changed in Page Setup.

In new versions of Excel, on the Page Layout tab on the ribbon, you can do many of these things without going into the Page Setup screen. For example, you will see an Orientation button. If you want to go into the Page Setup screen, simply click on the arrow (dialogue box launcher) at the bottom of the Page Setup group when you click on the Page Layout tab on the ribbon.

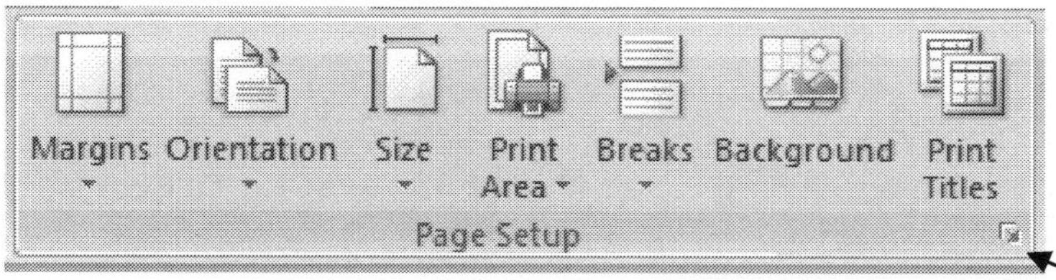

Dialogue Box Launcher

Page Tab

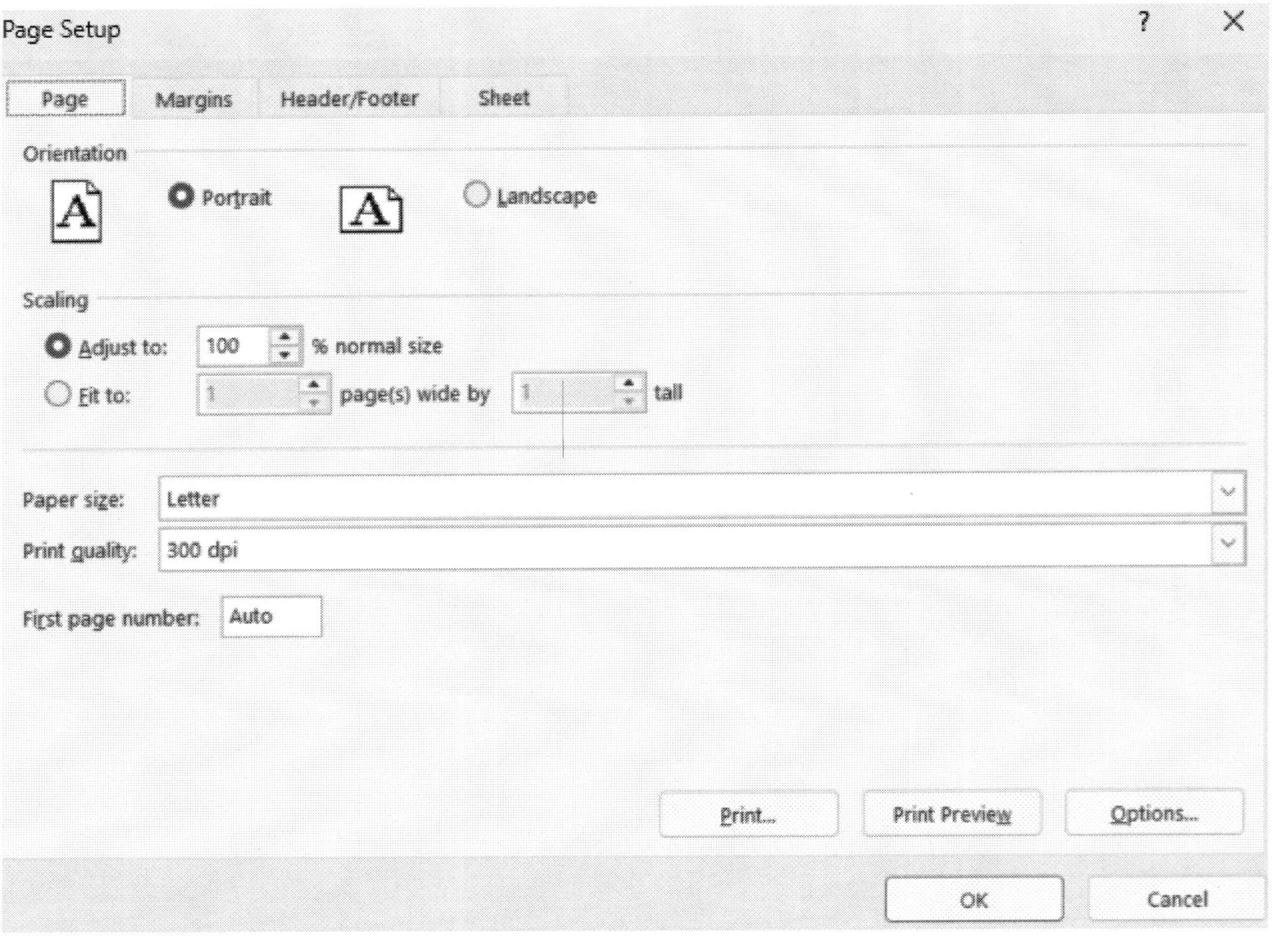

Orientation	Determines whether Excel prints in portrait (vertical) or landscape (horizontal) mode. Landscape is not available for all printers.
Scaling	Allows you to size the spreadsheet to fit onto the page.
Paper Size	Allows you to choose the size of paper to print the spreadsheet on.
Print Quality	Allows you to pick the quality of printing.
First Page Number	Allows you to type a number for the page numbering to start at.

Margins Tab

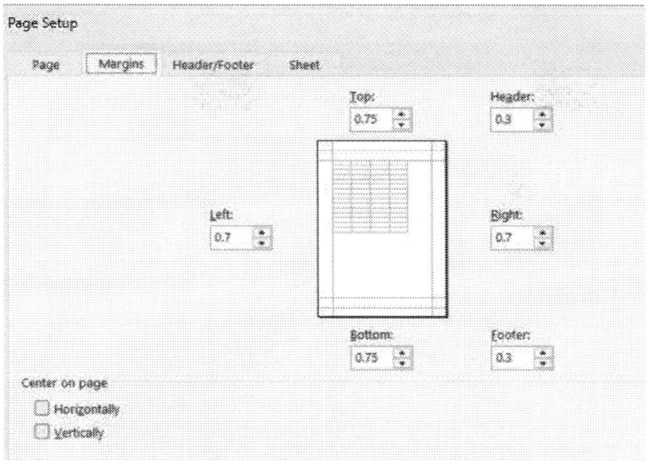

Top, Bottom, Left, Right	Specify the Left, Right, Top, Bottom Margins.
Header, Footer	Specify how close to the edge of the page to print the header and footer.
Center on Page	Lets you center the spreadsheet on the page either horizontally or vertically or both.

NOTE: You can also modify your margins while you're in Print Preview, you don't even need to be in the Page Setup box. Just click on the Show Margins button on the bottom right corner of the screen and you will be able to move the margins around yourself rather than typing in a dimension.

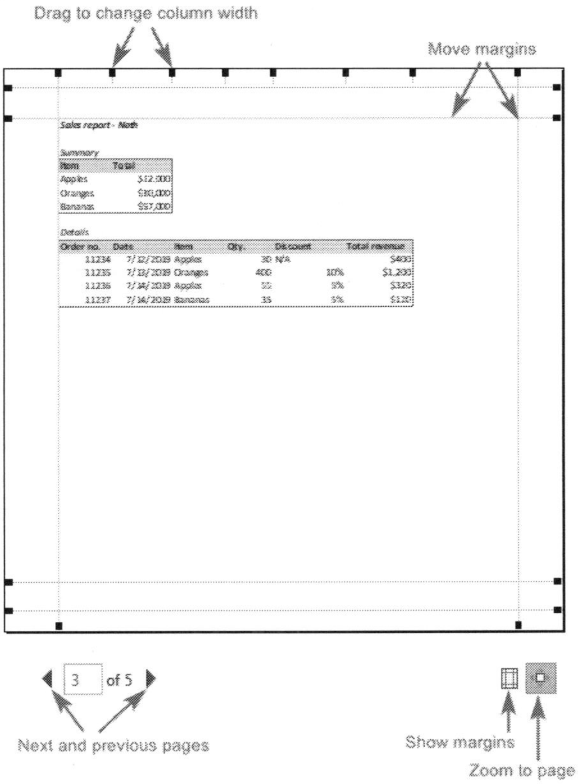

Header/Footer Tab

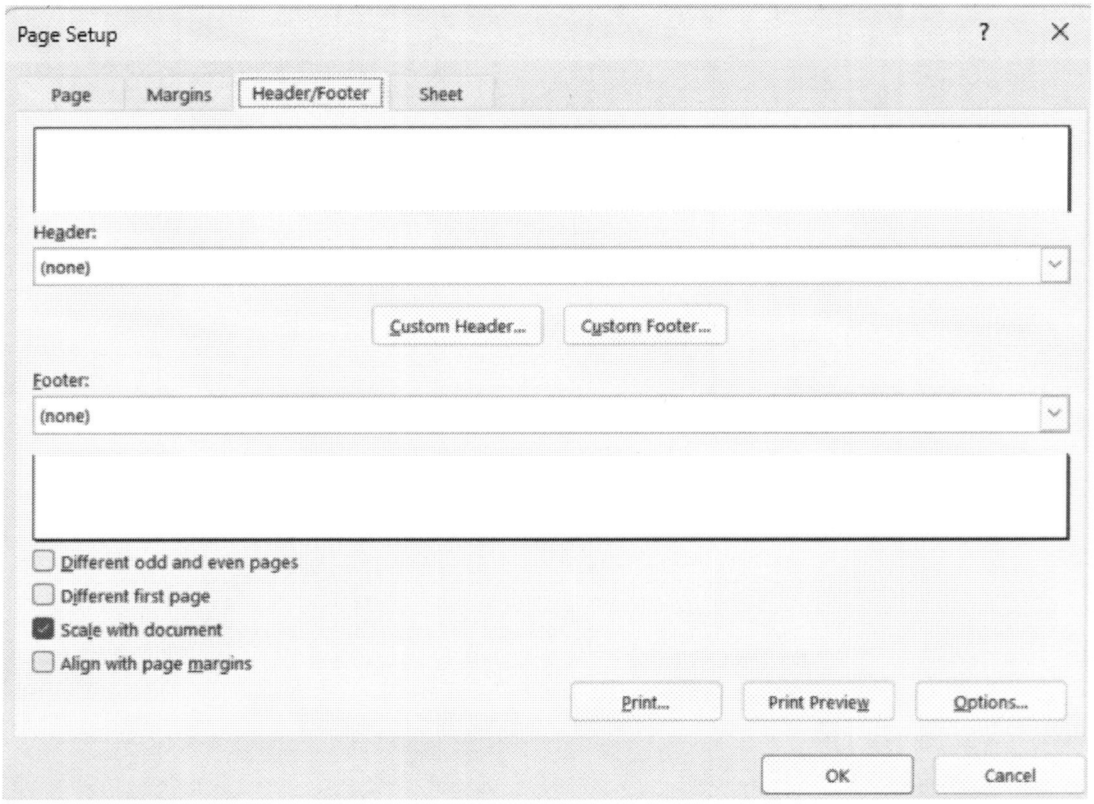

Header	Constant text at the top of the page. i.e. Company Name, Page #. You can pick a predefined header or create a custom one.
Footer	Constant text at the bottom of the page. i.e. Company Name, Page #. You can pick a predefined footer or create a custom one.

Adding a Page Number

1. If you would like a page number to appear on every page, click on the Custom Header or Footer button.
2. Position your cursor to where you want it displayed.
3. Type the word Page, if desired, and then click on the Page Number button.

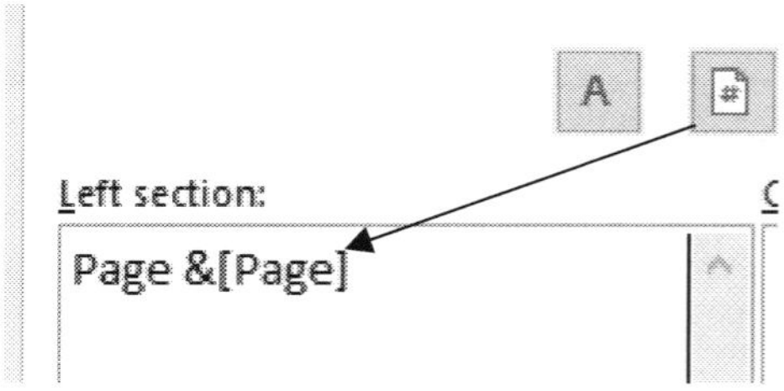

When creating a custom header or footer, you can insert special codes that will update every time it is printed. These special codes can be typed into the Custom Header or Footer or you can click on the tools that appear in the Header or Footer screen. If you click on the '**Custom Header**' or '**Custom Footer**', you will display the following dialog box:

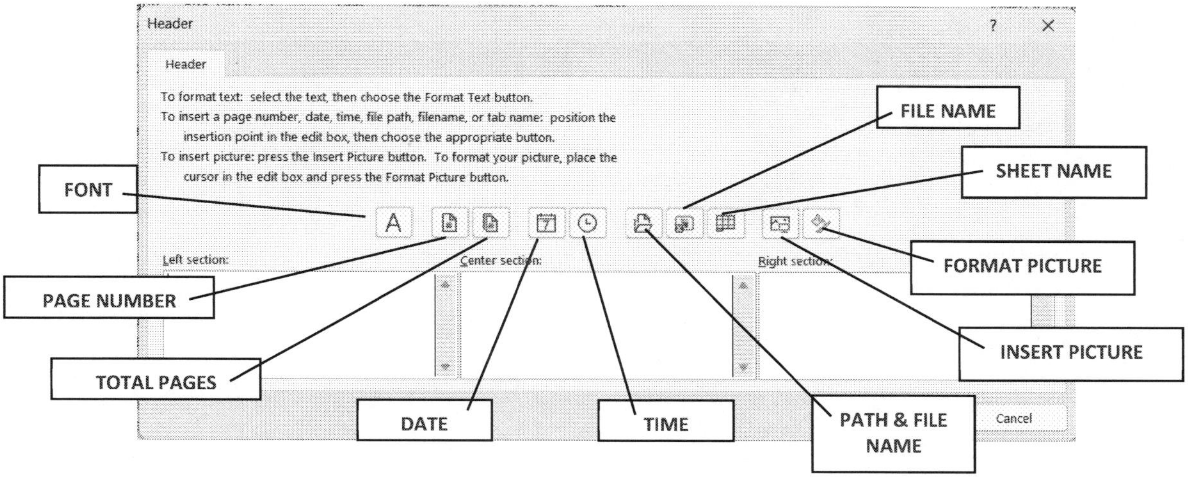

A		Displays the *Font* dialog box so you can adjust the font, size, and style of the text for each of the three sections of the header or footer
	&[Page]	Inserts the page number
	&[Pages]	Inserts the total number of pages
	&[Date]	Inserts the date
	&[Time]	Inserts the time
	&[File]	Inserts the filename of the workbook
	&[Tab]	Inserts the name of the current worksheet
	&[Path]&[File]	Inserts the path and filename (ie. c:\data\budget.xls)
	&[Picture]	Displays the *Insert Picture* dialog box so you can insert a picture
		Displays the *Format Picture* dialog box so you can adjust picture properties

You can also edit your headers and footers through the Page Layout View Tab on the bottom right corner of your screen.

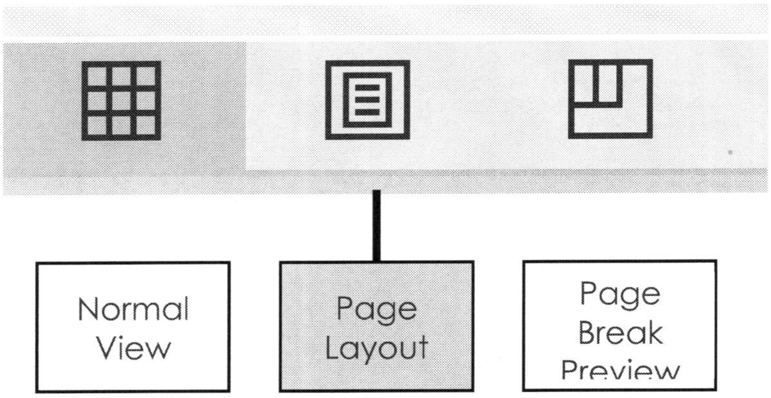

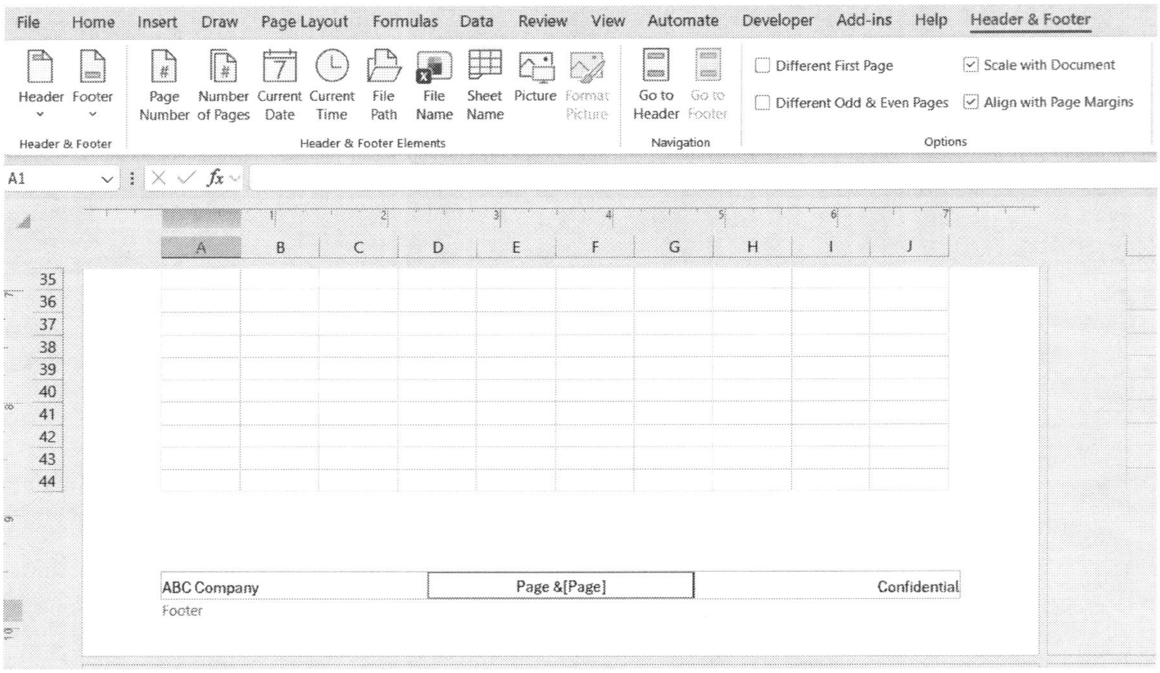

This allows you to click where you want to type in your header/footer and add useful codes to it such as page numbers and/or dates.

To get your screen back to normal, click on a cell within your spreadsheet and then click on the Normal View button.

Sheet Tab

Print Area	Allows you to define an area on the spreadsheet to print
Print Titles	Specifies the columns of worksheet data to print at the left of every page and print range and the rows of worksheet data to print at the top of every page and above every print range. NOTE: if you have added columns to repeat at left, it sometimes changes the scaling percent if you have set it to Fit All Columns on One Page so you may have to manually increase the percentage to take advantage of the space.
Print options	Allows you to choose to print gridlines, row and column headings and other options such as how to print comments, notes and cell errors
Page Order	Allows you to choose which order to print the pages if they happen to span across more than one page.

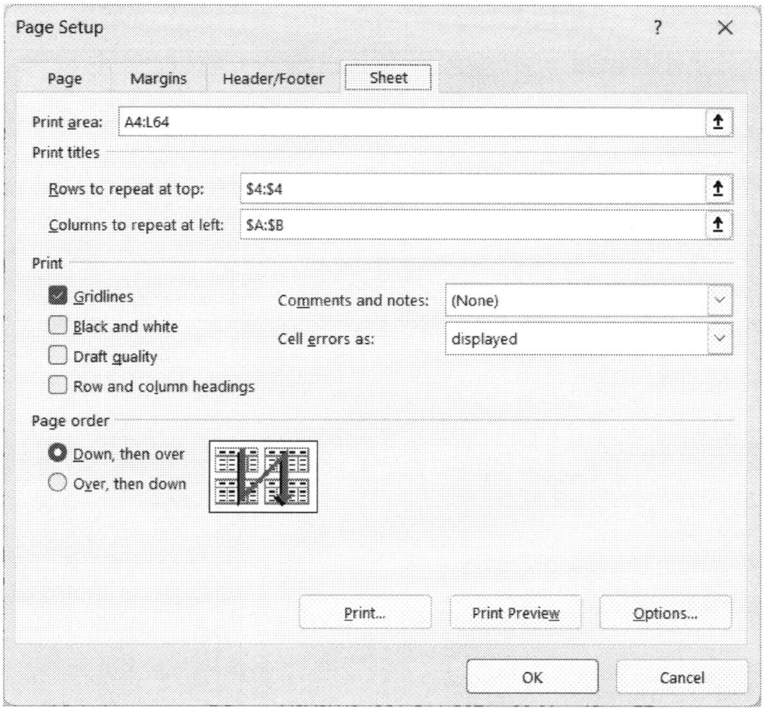

Printing the Worksheet

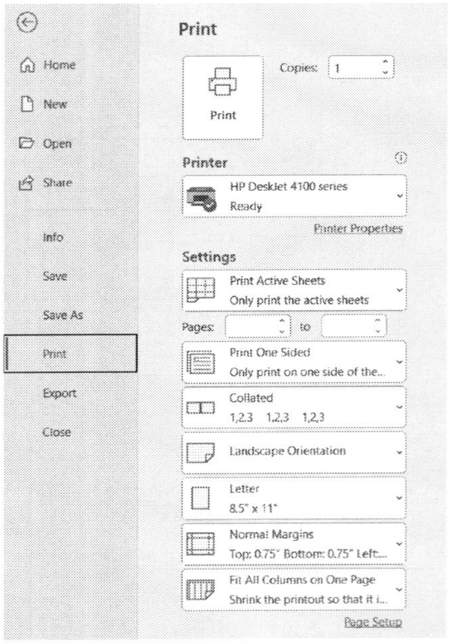

If you choose a print area in Page Setup, you can select Print Active Sheets (default) to print the range. If you didn't set a print range, Excel guesses at what to print. If you select a range before going into the Print menu, you can choose Selection. This overrides the specified print area. You also have the option to print all the sheets by choosing the Entire Workbook.

You can also choose how many copies to print and which pages.

1. Choose Print from the File menu.

Print Areas

You may choose to set up an area to print each time you print this spreadsheet or you may set up a one-time print area.

1. Temporary Print Area

   To print only a portion of the spreadsheet, simply select the area, and choose SELECTION from the **Print** menu under Settings. It likely displays Print Active Sheets as a default.

2. Permanent Print Area

   Method One:

   To choose an area to print, click on the SHEET tab from the **File Page Setup** menu.

   {Click} in the **Print Area** box and click and drag over the cells you want to print. You can also type the names of the cells in. When you choose **Print** from the file menu or the toolbar, this area will always print.

   Note: You must go into Page Setup from the Page Layout tab. You cannot access it from the Print screen to modify Print Area and Print Titles.

   Method Two:

   Choose Page Break Preview from the bottom right of your screen or from the View ribbon tab. Drag the blue lines around the cells you wish to print.

Print Titles

You can set your print titles if you have a long and/or wide spreadsheet and you need certain information repeated on every page.

An example is if you want to repeat the header row. You would choose the header rows as the Rows to Repeat at the top.

You may need to produce a list of employees or clients with their and age in a wide spreadsheet that has columns you don't want to print. You would set up the columns with the names in them as Columns to Repeat at the Left.

If you have that many columns of information, how will you ever all fit it on one page? You can flip your spreadsheet to print landscape and decrease your font size, but it would be really great if you could just select the columns you want to print and not worry about the other ones.

This is easily done with a few simple steps.

1. Start by typing all your information in, starting at column A. Make sure you separate first name from last name, this allows more flexibility later should you decide to merge a letter to your list of names.

	A	B	C	D	E	F	G	H	I	J	K	L
1												
2			COMMISSION	5.00%								
3												
4	LAST.NAME	FIRST.NAME	INVEST.AMT	COMMISSION	REP	ADDRESS	CITY	PROV	ZIP	SSN	BIRTH.DATE	AGE
5	Jones	Clem	23,530.00	1,176.50	Marty	858 Tarsir Ct.	Red Deer	AB	T4P0N9	964-728-476	16-Jul-42	83
6	Quooddalk	Clarissa	22,230.00	1,111.50	Marty	1421 Oak Ct.	Prince Albert	SK	S6Z2T2	997-798-704	11-Sep-63	62
7	Nitron	Monica	32,770.00	1,638.50	Lorie	435 Lonosphere St.	Regina	SK	S4J5R1	980-373-510	05-Feb-28	97
8	Butheez	Pixie	27,520.00	1,376.00	Gordon	1067 Arthropod Ct.	Prince George	BC	V2N5C3	996-218-120	03-Oct-50	75
9	Smoimeib	Sandy	3,640.00	182.00	Thomas	1484 Mesquite Rd.	Prince George	BC	V2R0D4	919-227-477	17-Aug-62	63
10	Zaultet	Maya	16,210.00	810.50	Thomas	1189 Maple Ct.	Fort McMurray	AB	T9M5T1	954-645-249	01-Jul-55	70

2. Click on the Page Layout tab and then Print Titles. This takes you directly to the Sheet tab within the Page Setup box. Here you will set up the rows and columns to print on every page. Later, you will select only the data you want to print and these corresponding rows and columns you choose on this screen will automatically print.

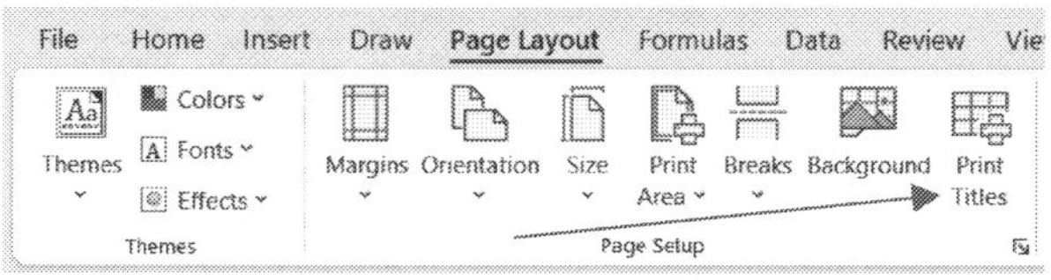

3. Click in the "Rows to Repeat at Top" text area.

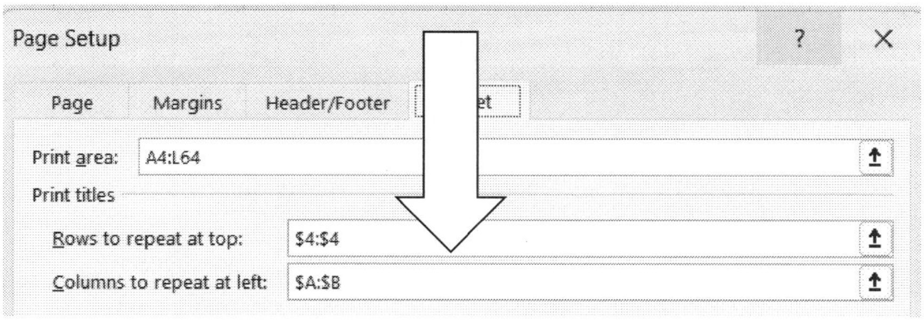

4. Next, click anywhere on the row that contains your heading row. This step is something you could do in all Excel spreadsheets in order to have this row repeat at the top of every page.

   You will see that the row number, along with some dollar signs appear. Don't let the dollar signs scare you, just ignore them!

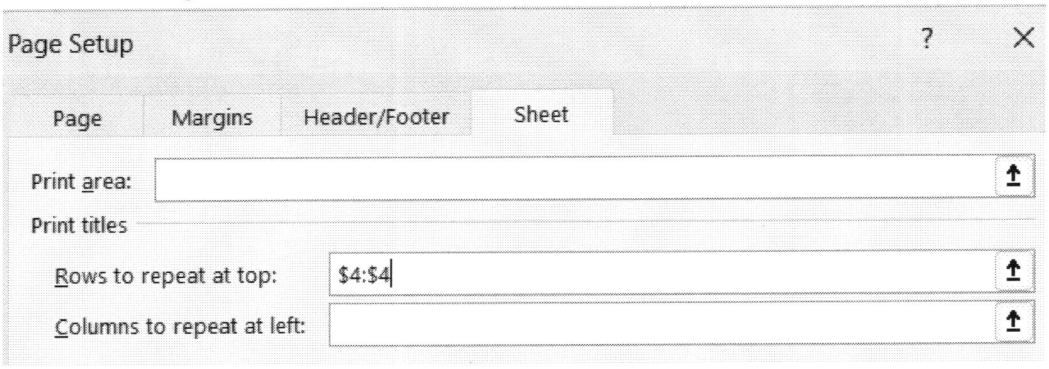

5. Now you will do the same with the columns. Click on the "Columns to Repeat at Left" text area and then click or click and drag in your spreadsheet where the column(s) you wish to always appear are. In our case, it is column A and B. This is the secret to making great reports in Excel!

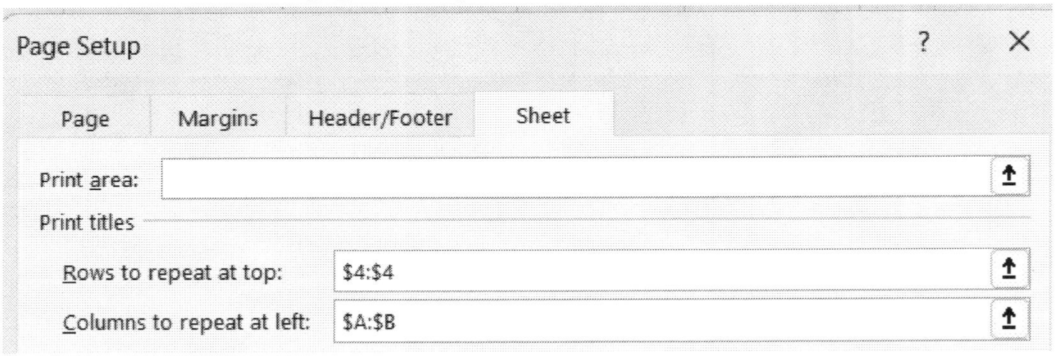

6. After you've clicked OK to save your changes, the rest is very simple.

   Simply select the cells you want printed, excluding the rows and columns you chose in the above steps.

   For example, if you want a list of names and ages, simply drag your mouse over all the ages.

K	L
BIRTH DATE	AGE
16-Jul-42	83
11-Sep-63	62
05-Feb-28	97
03-Oct-50	75
17-Aug-62	63
01-Jul-55	70
27-Dec-39	85
25-Oct-12	113
15-Jul-40	85
21-Mar-41	84
15-Apr-52	73
13-Jan-43	82
27-Dec-50	74
06-Mar-58	67
19-Jun-16	109
21-Aug-40	85
08-Apr-43	82

7. Now you're ready to print. Go into the File menu and choose Print. The trick here is to change it from "Print Active Sheets" to "Print Selection: to make it only print your print titles which you set up earlier and the selected cells.

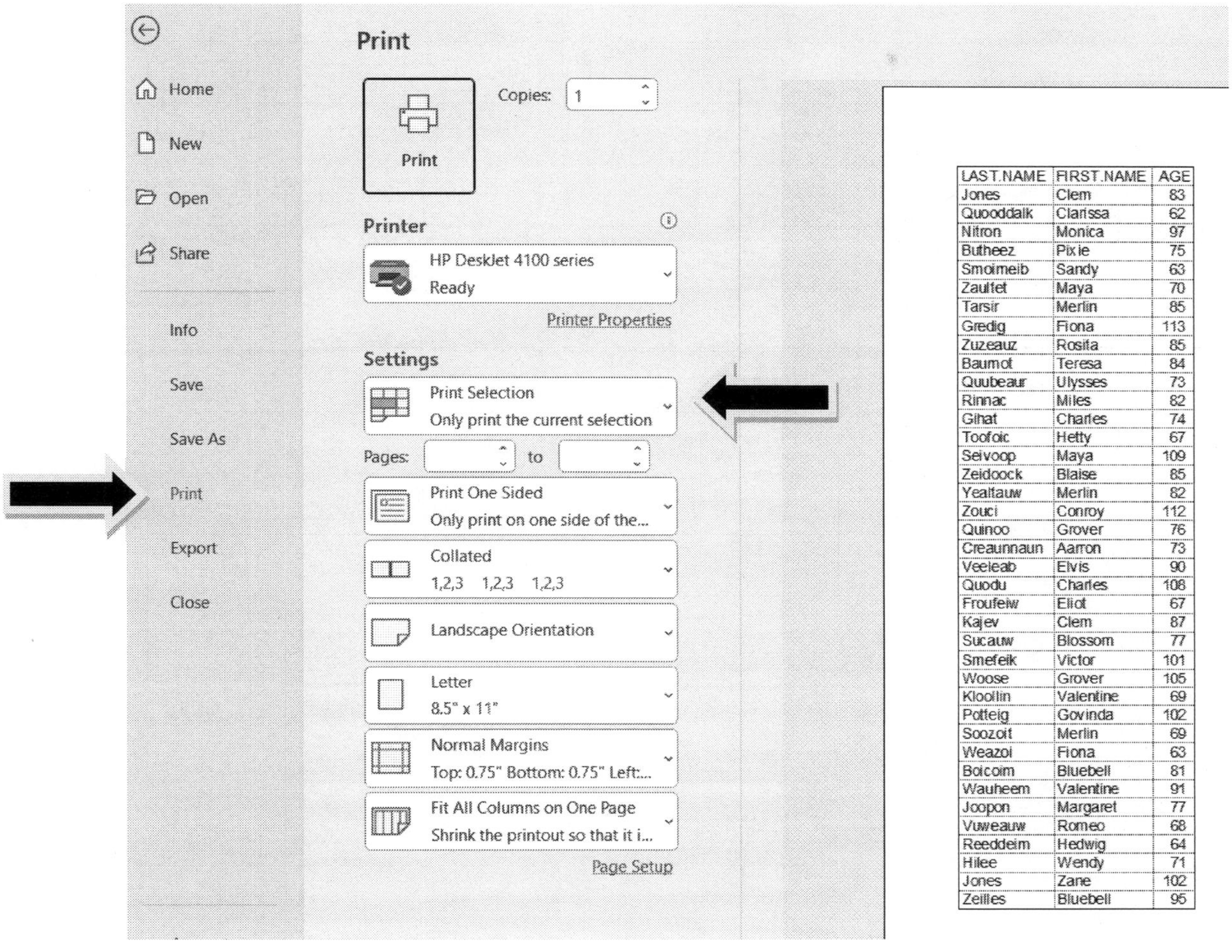

There you have it! Only the selected information prints with the print titles! Remember when setting up your spreadsheet, put like columns together so that you can print multiple columns this way.

Next time, you can select something different, say NAMES and CITY and repeat the above step. Another great list!

Exercise

Open 04X Printing Practice

Make each sheet look great. The instructions are in each sheet!

Excel Printing Cheat Sheet

#1 To Specify What to Print, Set your Print Area!

- Click on the Page Break Preview button on the bottom right corner of the screen.
- Drag the Solid Blue Lines to enclose the desired cells.
- To get back to Normal view, click Normal.

 # 2 To Add a Header/Footer

- Click Page Layout button on the bottom right of the screen and type the text in the desired spot.
- To get back to Normal view, click on a cell, then click Normal.

#3 To Add a Page Number

- Follow Above Steps for Header/Footer
- Type Page (if desired) and then click the Page # button on the Header/Footer toolbar

#4 To Print Selected Cells

- Select Cells
- File Print
- Choose Print Selection instead of Active Sheet

#5 To Flip it to Landscape or Portrait

- File, Print

OR

- Page Layout Tab at top of screen

#6 To Modify Margins

- File Print
- Click Margins to choose Predefined

OR

- Click Show Margins (Bottom Right)

#7 To Make it Fit Properly on the Page

- File, Print
- Change Scaling to Fit All Columns on One Page

#8 To Repeat Headings at the Top/Side of Each Page

- Click Print Titles on the Page Layout Tab at top of Screen
- Click beside "Rows/Columns to Repeat at the Top" and Click on the Row(s)/Column(s) to Repeat

PowerPoint

PowerPoint is a program that you can use to create presentation, picture slide shows and signs.

The Opening Screen

When you first run the program, you'll be presented with the following screen:

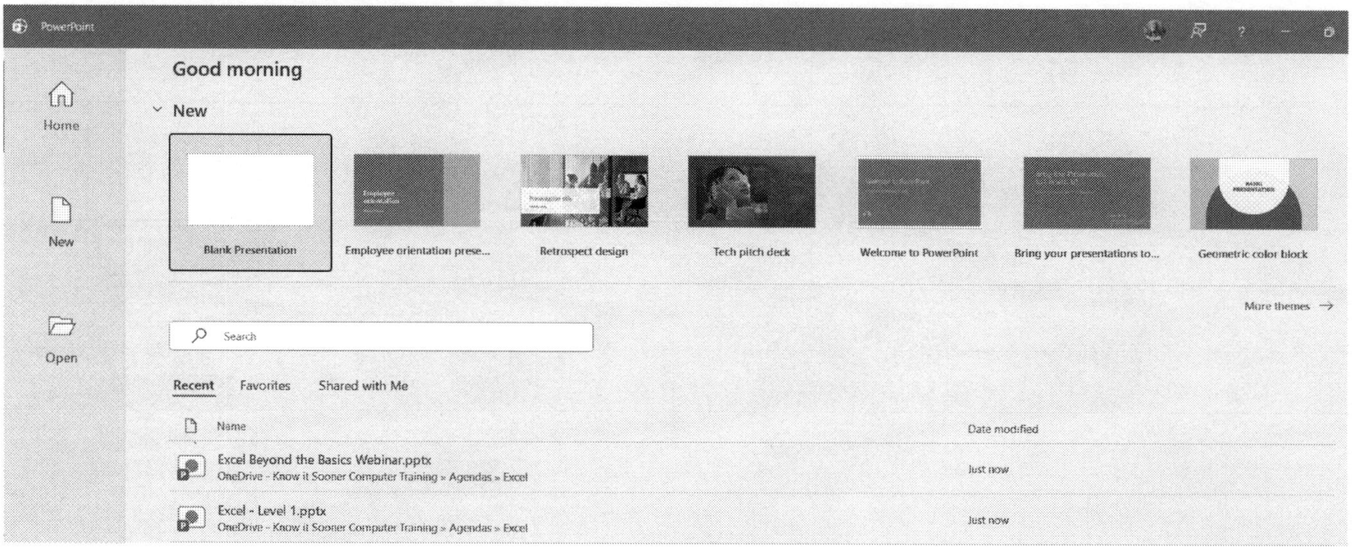

Notice you can open a recently used presentation, an older presentation that has been stored on your system, or you can create a new presentation based on of the many templates and themes available.

If you would like to create a presentation, you are able to select from one of the color schemes for that theme. And since most of the world's display has gone to widescreen and HD format, PowerPoint offers that option, with 16:9 being the new default slide size. However, you can change the size to 4:3 if you prefer – or another custom size.

If you don't see a template that matches the presentation you want to create, choose Blank Presentation.

The Powerpoint Screen

Once you are in a blank untitled presentation, you may begin entering your data.

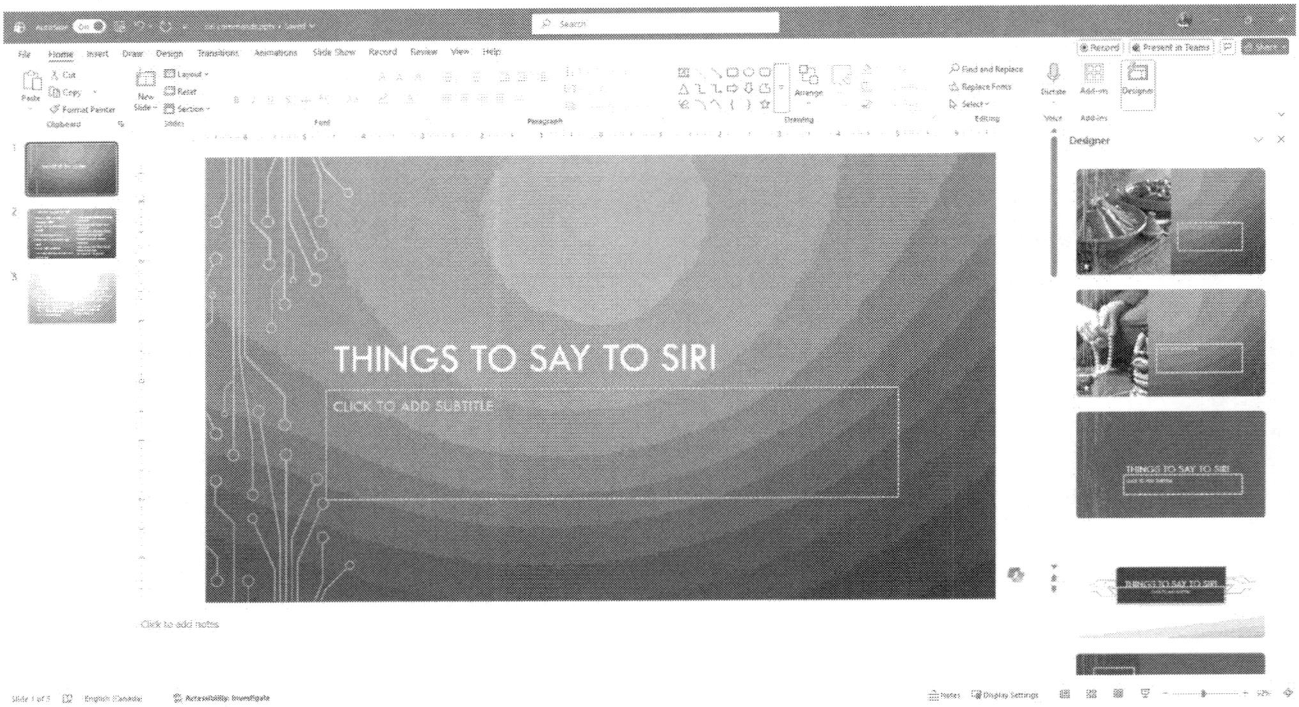

Along the top left corner of the screen is the **PowerPoint** button which is used to manipulate the program window (minimize, maximize and restore its size, move it, close it). To the right of the PowerPoint button is the Save tool as well as the Undo and Redo tools. Since those are tools that are most often used, they are placed in a convenient location on what is referred to as the "Quick Access Menu". Click on the button to the right of these tools to customize this Quick Access Menu.

The name of current presentation is displayed in the **Title Bar**.

Creating a Presentation

You can either create a presentation from scratch or use one of your own existing files to base the new presentation on. In addition, you can base the new presentation on one of PowerPoint's built-in templates. For example, if you want to create a marketing presentation, you could use PowerPoint's template and then edit it to include your specific information. Using a template can save you a great deal of preparation time.

To create a new presentation, select **New** from the File tab on the Ribbon.

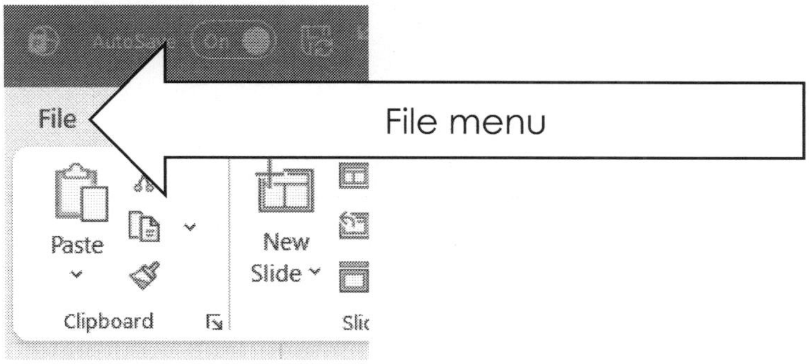

A window similar to this one will be displayed:

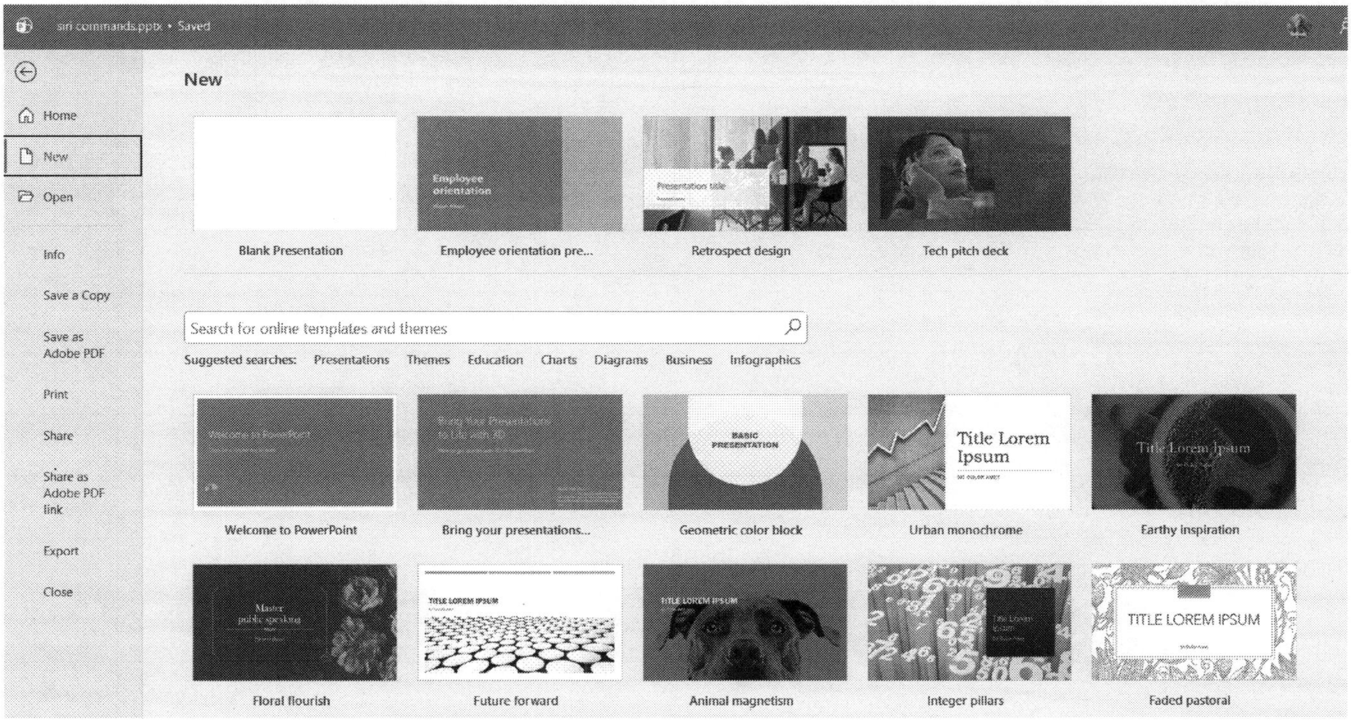

You can create a blank presentation or base the new file on one of the built-in templates that come with PowerPoint. A template is used to determine the basic structure of the presentation and can contain predefined settings, such as colors, fonts, layouts, graphics, formatting, and macros.

When you click on one of the templates, a pop-up window is displayed with a preview of the template and a short description.

If there are templates that you'll be using on a regular basis, you may want to pin them to the list so that they remain at the top for easy access.

To quickly pin a template, point to the template and then click on (located along the bottom right corner of its preview or click your [RIGHT] mouse button once and choose **Pin to list** from the pop-up menu).

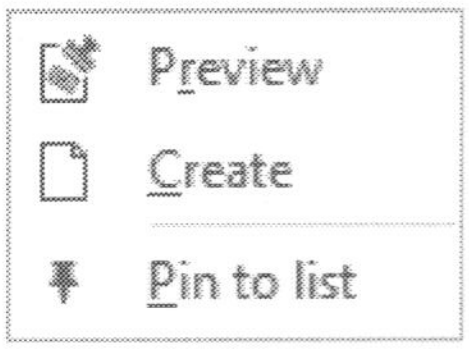

If you change your mind, click the icon (located on the template preview) to unpin the template.

If you decide you'd like to use the selected template, click on this button.

The new presentation will be created - based on the template you have selected.

> ***NOTE:*** *To quickly create a new blank presentation without first having to access the File menu, press CTRL N.*

Creating a Photo Album (Picture Slideshow)

To quickly create a picture slide show, you can create a Photo Album.

1. Start by putting all your pictures into a folder on your computer.
2. In the Insert Ribbon tab, click **Photo Album**.
3. Click Choose **File/Disk** and then choose the location of your folder that contains all the pictures.

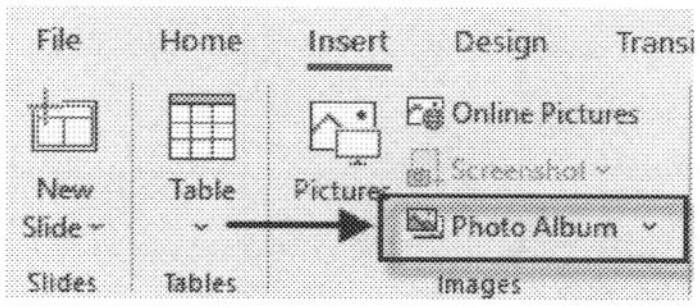

4. Next, click on one of the pictures listed, press CTRL A to select all the pictures in the folder. Click on **Insert**.
5. You can spend some time on this screen changing the layout, brightness, etc. or the order of them using the arrows.

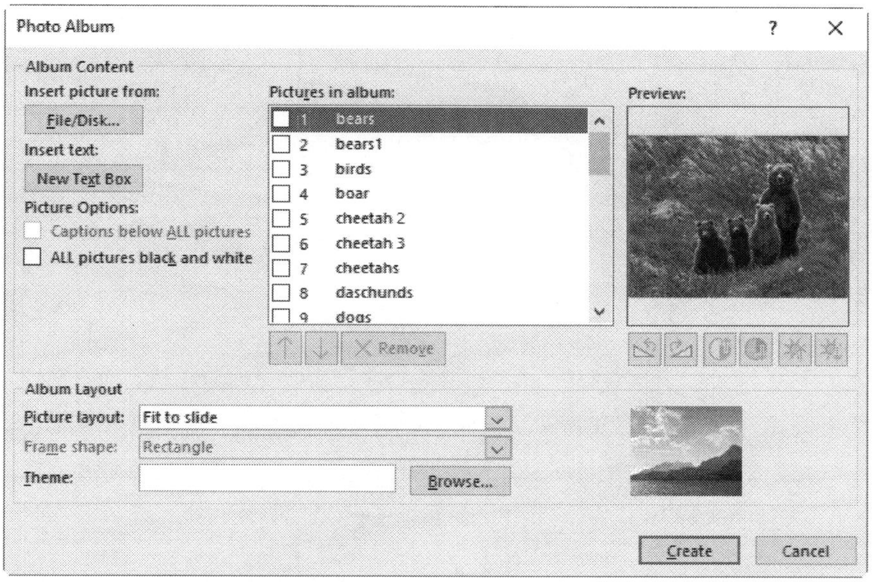

6. Click Create when finished. This will insert all your photos into the presentation.

If you want to edit the Photo Album, go into Insert Photo Album and choose Edit from the drop down list.

Changing Views

The PowerPoint screen is divided into three basic panes. The leftmost pane is most often used to display thumbnails of each slide within your presentation while the large middle pane displays the currently selected slide. The pane beneath the working area is used for adding and displaying slide notes.

To switch between the various views, PowerPoint offers a series of buttons located along the bottom right of the screen. Each view has its advantages.

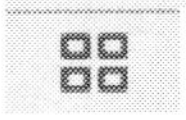

The **Notes** option allows you to quickly add notes to the current slide that can be printed.

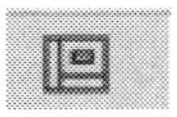

The **normal** view is normally used to show the thumbnail of the slide on the left side of the screen. If you click it again, it will switch the thumbnail to outline view so you can easily edit the text.

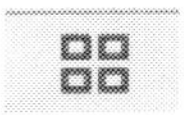

The **slide sorter** view is best used to view the entire presentation at once, rearrange the slides, copy and move slides between presentations and delete slides from the presentation.

The **reading** view is used to display the slide show within the current window size rather than a full screen.

The **slide show** view is best used to preview your presentation to verify the timing and transition methods between slides.

Changing the Viewing Size

Along the status bar (just to the right of the viewing icons) is the **Zoom** area. Notice you can click on the increase **+** or decrease **-** buttons to change the zoom factor.

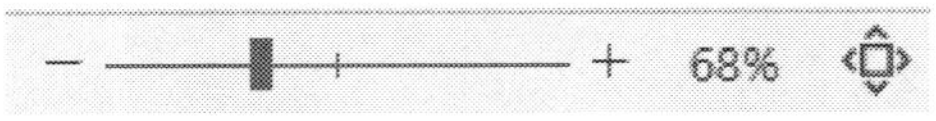

You can also drag the slider horizontally to change the slide size as it appears on the screen. PowerPoint displays the current percentage just to the left of this area.
tip

The button on the right besides the percent will shrink or expand the slide to fit perfectly on the screen so you can edit everything about it!

Try holding the CTRL key down while you scroll with the wheel on the mouse to zoom in and out!

Working Within the Slide Pane

Since the slide pane is set as the largest pane within PowerPoint, it is important that you understand the screen elements present when working within this pane.

Notice along the bottom left side of the screen (on the status bar) that PowerPoint indicates the current slide number.

Along the bottom right side of the slide (on the vertical scroll bar) are two buttons which can be used to quickly move to the previous and next slide within the presentation.

Along the right side of the slide, PowerPoint displays a vertical scroll bar which can be used to move to specific slides.

Drag the rectangular scroll box up or down to display the desired slide number/name.

Notice as you drag, that a small text box shows the number and title of the slide that would be displayed if you were to release the mouse button.

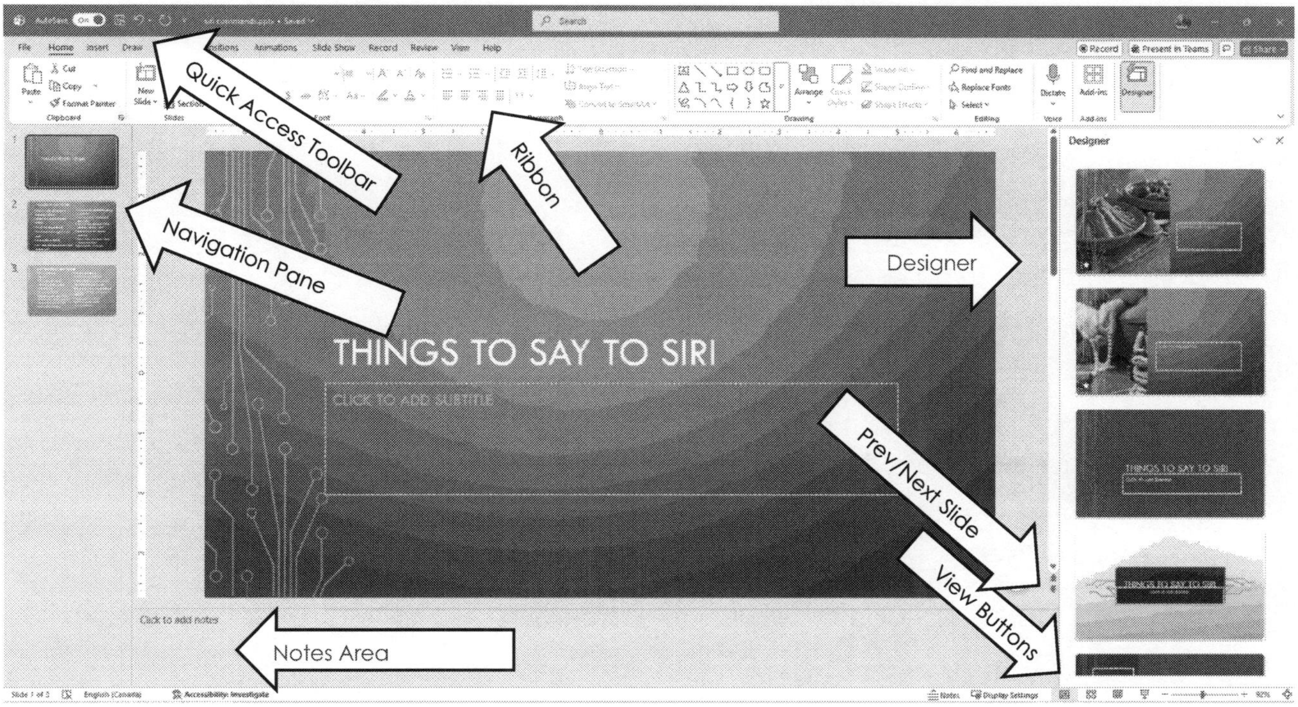

Inserting a Slide

1. Click the **New Slide** button (the lower part with the dropdown arrow) from the **Home** tab on the ribbon
2. Select your desired layout from the gallery that appears

Quick method: Press **CTRL** **M** to instantly insert a new slide with the default layout (usually Title and Content).

Understanding Slide Layouts

PowerPoint offers several built-in layouts to organize your content. Here is an explanation of some of the common ones:

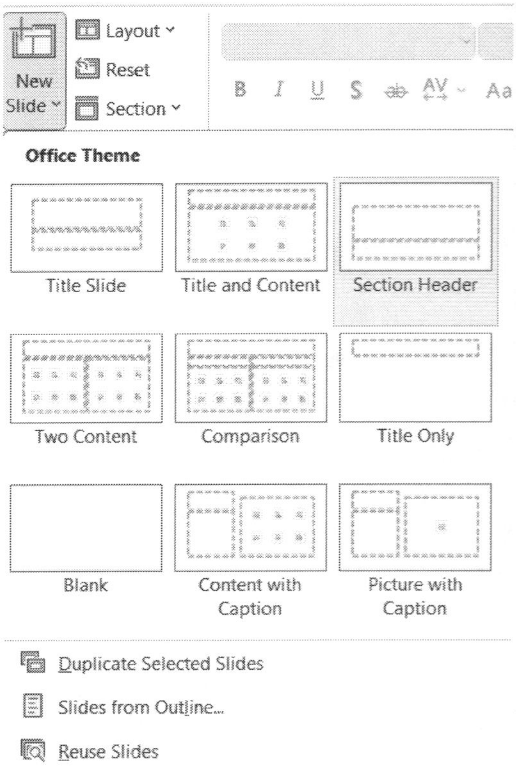

- Title Slide - Designed for your opening slide with a main title and subtitle
- Title and Content - The most commonly used layout, with a title at the top and a content area below for text, images, or other objects
- Section Header - Similar to Title Slide but formatted for introducing new sections within your presentation
- Two Content - Features a title with two side-by-side content areas, ideal for comparisons
- Comparison - Two content areas with separate headings above each
- Title Only - Just a title placeholder, giving you maximum space for custom content
- Blank - No placeholders at all, providing complete freedom for your design
- Content with Caption - Large content area on one side with text space on the other
- Picture with Caption - Optimized for featuring an image with descriptive text

Changing the Layout After Insertion

If you need to switch to a different layout:

1. Select the slide you want to change (click on it in the slide thumbnail pane)
2. Go to the **Home** tab
3. Click **Layout** in the Slides group
4. Choose your new layout from the gallery

Your existing content will adjust to fit the new layout's placeholders where possible.

Outlining your Presentation

USAGE: Use the outline pane (located to the left of the slide) to start the "brainstorming" portion of your presentation.

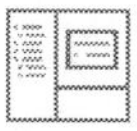

Outline View

Click this icon (located on the View Ribbon) to access the Outline View.

This pane is great for quickly creating new slides, rearranging slides or entering the bullet items for a slide. Entering text is also easiest through the use of the outline.

TIP:  *To increase the size of the outline pane, place the mouse pointer on the vertical line separating the slide and outline pane. The pointer will change to a 2-way arrow ⇔. Hold down the **[LEFT]** mouse button and drag the mouse right to increase the outline pane.*

To the left of each title is the slide number and slide icon. The slide number indicates the order in which the slide will be displayed within the presentation.

Promoting/Demoting Topics

When working with slides containing bullet or number lists, you can change the outline level of a particular item by promoting/demoting it. Promoting an item refers to raising its hierarchy level within the outline by outdenting the item. Demoting refers to lowering an item's hierarchy level within the outline by indenting the item.

1. Click at the end of a line and press [ENTER]
2. Then press [TAB] to demote a topic or press [SHIFT]+[TAB] to promote a topic.
   If you don't press [TAB], you will be at the same "level" and it will look like the line above it.
3. Type your text.
4. Repeat step 1!

Working with the Slide Sorter

The **Slide Sorter** displays a thumbnail sketch of each of your slides so that you can easily see them all at once. These miniature slides are spread across several rows on a single screen (whenever possible).

This view is the quickest way to move slides around and delete unwanted slides.

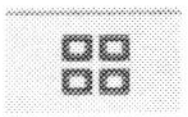

Click this button (located with the other view buttons along the bottom right side of the screen) to access the **Slide Sorter** view.

The outline/slide pane closes to expand the working area so that you can display several slides at once, as shown below:

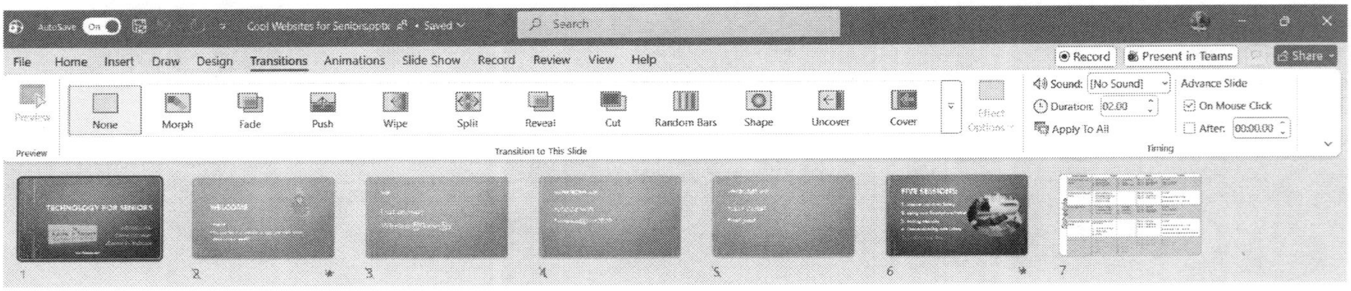

Rearranging Slides

You can rearrange the slides within the slide sorter by simply dragging them to a new location. As you begin dragging a slide, a thin vertical line is displayed to indicate where the slide will be placed when you release the mouse button.

Adding Slide Transitions

By clicking the Transitions ribbon tab at the top, you can choose different ways to advance the slides during the slide show.

1. Select one or more slides.
2. Click on one of the transition buttons. You can also set a specific time to display the slide during the actual slide show.

If you want to select more than one slide in order:
(for example, you want to select from slide 4-10)

- Click on the first one (slide 4)
- Hold down the SHIFT key
- Click on the last slide (slide 10)
- Release the SHIFT key

If you want to select more than one slide:

- Click on the first slide you want
- Hold down the CTRL key to select others
- Release the CTRL key

If you want to select all the slides:

- Click on any of the slides
- Press CTRL A

Running a Slide Show

A slide show is a desktop presentation. They are most often used when presenting information to an audience. Slide shows can be instrumental in conveying your message to a group of people since graphics can help make it more understandable.

You can connect your PC to an overhead projector or big screen TV and display the show to a large group of people or it can be used on the PC in front of a small group (i.e., a sales presentation). It can either be running in the background as you speak to the group or you can add enough special effects and sound that the show itself is sufficient in conveying the point you are trying to make, such as a picture slide show.

It is possible to control the flow of the show using either the keyboard or the mouse. It can be a self-running demonstration or can run interactively with the audience depending on your requirements. You can also change the sequence of the slides in the middle of the show if needed.

Running a slide show will display each of the slides contained within a presentation file one at a time on the computer screen. You can determine an **automatic** time interval between slides being drawn on the screen or you can instruct PowerPoint that you want to **manually** determine the speed each of the slides is drawn.

If you run it manually, you can use the mouse or keyboard to move between slides.

Another nice feature is the ability to **Rehearse** the times between slides by previewing the show and setting individual times for each slide of the presentation.

Starting a Slide Show

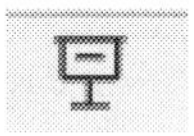

Click this tool (located with the view buttons – towards the right side of the status bar).

PowerPoint will immediately begin displaying the slide you're currently on full screen.

Press the F5 key to automatically start the slide show from the first slide!

Using the Pen

By default, when you click the **[LEFT]** mouse button while viewing a slide show, the next slide within the presentation will be displayed. However, if you prefer, you can assign a pen or highlighter to the **[LEFT]** mouse button to emphasize points as the show is running.

To do so, click your **[RIGHT]** mouse button (from within the slide show) and choose "Pointer Options" from the pop-up menu.

You can also click on the  tool (which is located with the other slide show tools along the bottom left of your slide show screen).

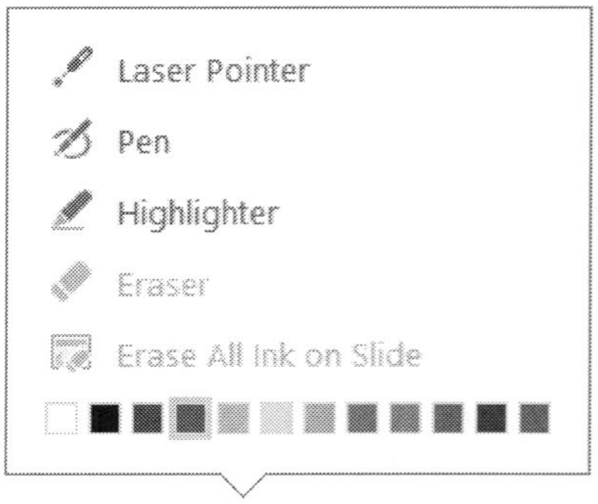

A pop-up menu will be displayed.

Select the type of pen or highlighter you would like to use to annotate your slides during the show.

Notice you can also choose a different **Ink Color**. The default color is black but you can choose any other color from the list provided.

After selecting a pen or highlighter, the function of the **[LEFT]** mouse button will have changed so that you may now begin annotating the slides during the show.

Once the pen or highlighter has been enabled, you will need to use the arrow tools (located with the other slide show tools along the bottom left side of the slide show screen) to move to the next or previous slide.

If you realize you have added too many annotations with the pen or highlighter, you can erase them by clicking the  tool or pressing E on your keyboard.

From the pop-up menu, choose **Erase All Ink on Slide** to erase all annotations you have added to the slide or select **Eraser** to manually erase only some of the annotations from the slide. If you choose the Eraser option, the pointer will change to an eraser so that you can click and drag to erase the unwanted marks.

To disable the pen or eraser, click on  and choose **Arrow** from the pop-up menu.

TIP:	*A quick way of resetting the **[LEFT]** mouse button to a normal pointer is to simply press the* **ESC** *key once.*

Notes Page View

The **Notes Page** view displays the actual slide in the top half of the screen and then leaves an area at the bottom for speaker notes. These notes can be printed as a reference for the speaker to help them with the presentation as they deliver it or can be left blank and handed out to the audience so that they can write their own comments as the presentation is being delivered.

To switch Notes Page view on and off, click this button (located along the status bar at the bottom of your screen).

The screen changes to display the slide with an area at the bottom for notes, as shown in the diagram below:

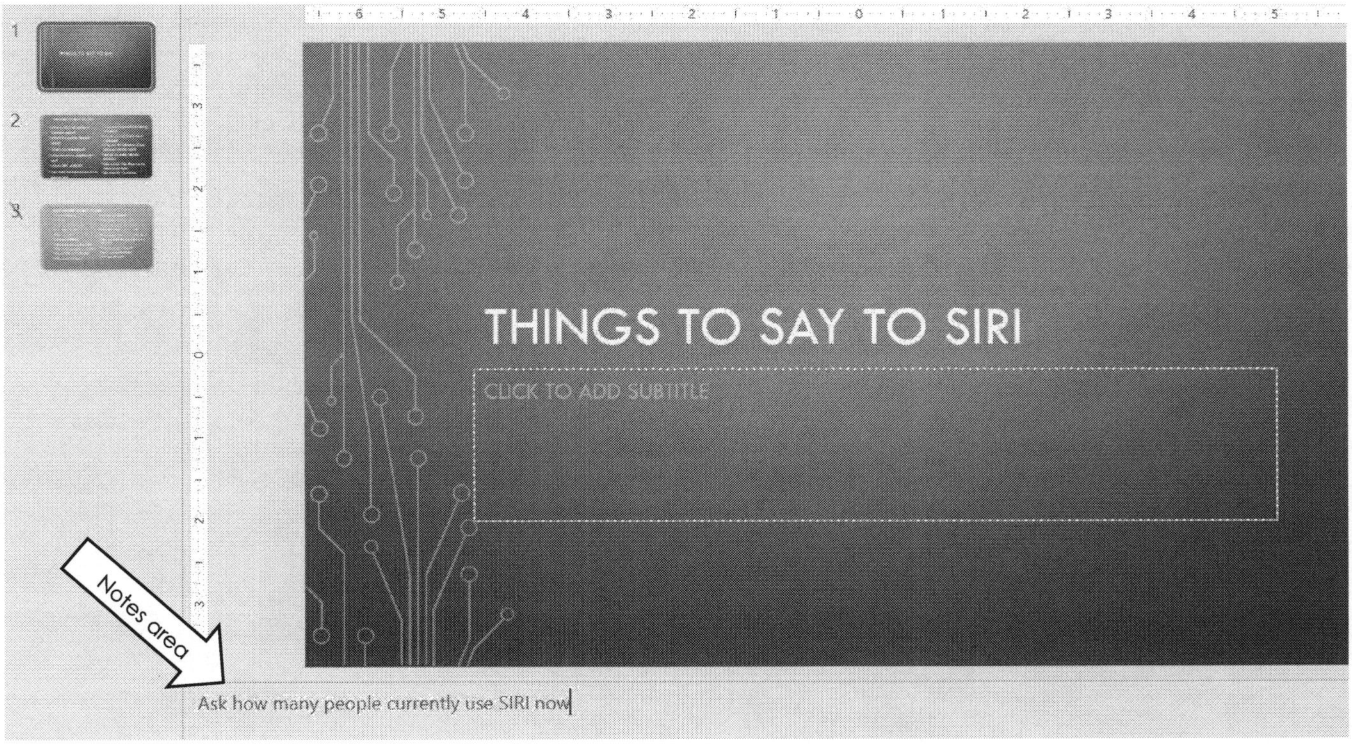

Before entering your notes, you might want to switch to a larger viewing size by clicking on the increase **+** button (located just to the right of the current zoom factor **100%** along the bottom right side of the screen).

Spell Checking a Presentation

Before finalizing a presentation, you should take advantage of PowerPoint's spell checking feature.

Not only does it check for misspellings, but it also will alert you of repeated words and incorrect capitalization.

The program comes with a main dictionary but you can add words to your own personal dictionary.

Click the **Spelling** button (located within the **Proofing** section on the Review Ribbon).

The following panel is opened along the right side of the screen:

PowerPoint will stop at the first unrecognized word, highlight it, and offer suggestions.

The following buttons are provided within the spell checking panel:

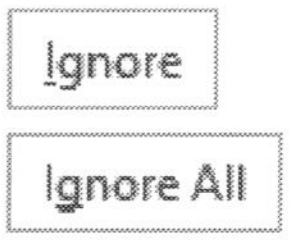

If the word should remain as it is, select the **Ignore** button. PowerPoint also offers the option of **Ignore All** if the word in question appears throughout the presentation.

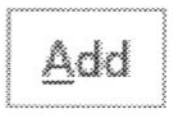

If the word should be added to your custom dictionary for future reference, click on this button.

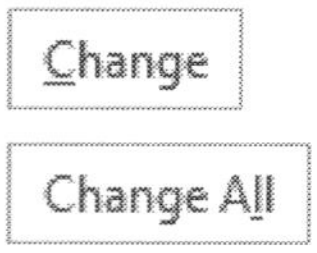

If one of the suggestions is correct, double-click on the correct spelling or highlight the word and choose the **Change** button. If you are afraid you misspelled a word more than once, click the **Change All** button.

Along the bottom half of the panel, PowerPoint provides an option to pronounce the selected word by clicking on this icon.

Notice that PowerPoint also provides a list of synonyms for the currently selected word.

Click this button to remove the panel from the screen.

After running the spell checker, you will want to save your presentation with all of the corrections.

Shortcut Keys

In Slide or Outline View:

KEYS:	ACTION:
CTRL + A	Select All
CTRL + B	Bold
CTRL + C	Copy
CTRL + D	Duplicate Slide or Object
CTRL + E	Center
CTRL + F	Find
CTRL + H	Find & Replace
CTRL + I	Italics
CTRL + J	Justify
CTRL + K	Insert a Hyperlink
CTRL + M	Insert a New Slide
CTRL + L	Left Align
CTRL + N	New Presentation
CTRL + O	Open a File
CTRL + P	Print
CTRL + R	Right Align
CTRL + S	Save
CTRL + T	Customize Font
CTRL + U	Underline
CTRL + V	Paste
CTRL + W	Close File
CTRL + X	Cut
CTRL + Z	Undo
CTRL + SPACEBAR	Clear Character Formatting

OUTLINE VIEW

Create a new line	ENTER
Demote the level	TAB →
Promote the level	SHIFT + TAB ←
Move a paragraph up/down	ALT SHIFT ↑/ ALT SHIFT ↓

SLIDE SHOW VIEW

Next Slide	→, ↓ N, ENTER, SPACEBAR or PG↓
Previous Slide	←, ↑ P, ←BACKSPACE or PG↑
End a slide show	ESC
Change the arrow to a pen	CTRL P
Change the pen to an arrow	CTRL A
Erase drawing on the screen	E
Stop or Restart an automatic slide show	S
Black out the screen	B
White out the screen	W
Go to specific slide	# followed by ENTER
Display list of controls	F1

OTHERS

Grouping	SHIFT Click on each object
Slide Show from Current Slide	SHIFT F5
Slide Show from Slide 1	F5

Typing Log

Go to a Browser such as Google Chrome and type www.typing.com in the address bar. You will see choices to do a typing test or a typing lesson. Record the results from your daily typing test below.

Date	Words Per Minute	Accuracy

Made in the USA
Monee, IL
08 November 2026

68108557R00071